Welcome to the course

Welcome to Modern World History! Studying this subject will help you to understand the world you live in: the events of the last hundred years can help to explain the problems and opportunities that exist in the world today.

How to use this book

There are four units in the course and each is worth 25% of the whole GCSE. This book covers Unit 3C: A divided union? The USA 1945-70. There are four key topics in this unit and you will study *all four*.

Key Topic 1: McCarthyism and the Red Scare

Key Topic 2: The civil rights movement 1945-62

Key Topic 3: Changes in the civil rights movement 1963-70

Key Topic 4: Other protest movements in the 1960s

exam zone

Zone in: how to get into the perfect 'zone' for revision.

Planning zone: tips and advice on how to plan revision effectively.

Know zone: the facts you need to know, memory tips and exam-style practice for every section.

Don't panic zone: last-minute revision tips.

Exam zone: what to expect on the exam paper.

Zone out: what happens after the exams.

ResultsPlus

Top Tips provide examiner advice and guidance to help improve your results.

> **ResultsPlus**
> **Top Tip**
>
> Political cartoons often have a message and show the views of the cartoonist about political issues. Students will do well if they work out the *message* from the content of the cartoon rather than just describe what is in the cartoon.

> **ResultsPlus**
> **Watch out!**
>
> Students can get confused about some civil rights terms. *Segregation* is keeping black and white people separate – its supporters are sometimes called separationists. *Integration* is having black and white people living or working together.

Watch out! These warn you about common mistakes and misconceptions that examiners frequently see students make.

Build better answers give an opportunity to answer exam-style questions. They include tips for what a basic or incorrect ■, good ● and excellent △ answer will contain.

> **ResultsPlus**
> **Build Better Answers**
>
> Some questions ask you to consider the *utility* of a source.
>
> ■ **Basic answers (level 1)** give a comment on usefulness, but do not provide detailed support.
>
> ● **Good answers (level 2)** consider what the source is for and its limitations.
>
> Exc... ...wers (level 3) consider the

Maximise your marks are featured in the Know Zone at the end of each section. They include an exam-style question with a student answer, examiner comments and an improved answer so that you can see how to build a better response.

> **ResultsPlus**
> **Maximise your marks**
>
> **Question 1**
> **Examiner's tip:** question 1 will ask you what you can learn about a particular topic from the sources provided. Be careful not to just copy information from the source. You need to make inferences from the sources – work something out based on the information in them. Let's look at an example (Source C on page 13).
>
> 'What can you learn from Source C about attitudes to McCarthy in 1951?' (6 marks)
>
> | Student answer | Examiner comment |
> |---|---|
> | The source tells me thousands listened to his speeches and millions of people thought he was a splendid American. On the other hand, it also tells me that there were people who thought McCarthyism was worse than communism. The New York Times quote said he was not a help in catching communists. | This answer mainly reproduces information from the source and would get very few marks. Let's rewrite the answer, making inferences and showing how the source helped us make them. |
> | ...... | In this answer there are several inferences made |

Unit 3: The source enquiry: an introduction

What is Unit 3 about?

The Unit 3 topics are very different from those in Units 1 and 2. To start with, you are never going to be asked to just recall historical information you have learned. If you find yourself sitting in an examination telling the story of what happened in a particular historical event, you are almost certainly doing it wrong! Unlike Units 1 and 2, Unit 3 is not about recalling or describing key features. Nor is it about using your knowledge to construct an argument about why things happened – or what the consequences of an action were. Instead, Unit 3 topics are about understanding the importance of sources in the study of history.

History as a subject is not just about learning a series of facts and repeating them in an examination. It is actually a process of enquiry. Historians understand that our historical knowledge comes from evidence from the past ('sources'). Historians have to piece together what has happened in the past from these sources. They need to interpret the sources to build up the historical picture. That is what you will be looking at in Unit 3.

Since sources can sometimes be interpreted in a number of ways, historians also have to make judgements about the usefulness of information in sources (utility) and whether these sources are giving us an accurate picture (reliability).

Of course, you cannot interpret sources or make judgements about their utility or reliability unless you know about the topic they relate to. That is why you do have to use your knowledge in an examination. You don't use it to tell the story, but you do use it to make judgements about sources. So for your Unit 3 topic, make sure you learn your information, but even more importantly, make sure you use it to make judgements about the sources. There are no marks in this unit for factual recall!

The examination

In the examination you will be given a collection of six to eight sources to study. Then you will be asked five questions. These five questions will test your understanding of interpreting sources. The good news is that each year the individual questions will always test the same skill. So question 1 will always be about making an inference. The table at the top of the next page shows how this works.

Question	Marks	Type of question
1	6	Making inferences from sources
2	8	Considering the purpose of a source
3	10	Cross-referencing sources
4	10	Evaluating the utility or reliability of sources
5	16	Evaluating a hypothesis

So before you study the historical topic from which your sources will be drawn, let's make sure you know how to answer each question type.

Making inferences from sources

When you read or look at a source and you understand its content, you are 'comprehending' that source. When you make a judgement from what the source says or shows, that is 'making an inference'. Let us look at a source to see what that means.

Source A
From a book about the USA in the 1960s.

> Some members of the SDS [a student protest society] went to Vietnam and came back praising the 'fearlessness calm determination and pride' shown by the Vietnamese revolutionaries confronting the world's greatest superpower. Viet Cong flags began to appear in anti-war demonstrations and marchers chanted slogans like 'Ho, Ho, Ho Chi Min the NFL [Vietnamese rebels] are gonna win!'

Read Source A. In the examination, the sort of question you might be asked would be:

'What can you learn about student protest from this source?'

You could say: *'they marched and chanted'*. That is true, but it doesn't take much working out, does it? It isn't an inference either, because that is exactly what the source says. An inference would be: *'Students were against the war in Vietnam and some of them even openly showed support for the revolutionaries that the USA was fighting'*. Can you see the difference?

Considering the purpose of a source

It is important for historians to understand why sources have been created. Sometimes people are just recording what has happened (as in a diary), but sometimes they are created to get a message across. For example, when a cartoonist sits down with a blank sheet of paper and draws a cartoon, he or she is doing so in order to get a message across. Let's look at an example.

A cartoon published in a US newspaper in 1967.

"THERE'S MONEY ENOUGH TO SUPPORT BOTH OF YOU ---- NOW, DOESN'T THAT MAKE YOU FEEL BETTER?"

In the examination, the sort of question you might be asked about this cartoon is:

'What was the purpose of this cartoon?'

You could say: *'to comment on the Vietnam War'*, but that is a poor answer. A good answer would be to look at the detail in the cartoon and work out why those things are there. The man in the cartoon is President Johnson, representing the US administration. He's talking to a woman in rags labelled 'US urban needs' and he's telling her there is enough money to support her and the other woman, labelled 'Vietnam War.' But one woman is in rags, the other very well dressed, so the message of the cartoon is that the US administration is spending too much on the war and the purpose of the cartoon is to get people to disapprove of the war.

Cross-referencing sources

Question 3 will ask you to compare three sources by looking at the information within them. Let us use our two previous sources and add a third to work out what this means. (Though you are more likely to be asked about three sources in the examination.)

Said by a student protester in an interview in 1970.

I reject everything my father stands for. I do not want to gear my life to making money. I do not want to get ahead. I do not have his patriotism for a nation that can't behave decently. I don't believe in the military, the Republican Party or the First National Bank.

In the examination, the sort of question you might be asked is:

'*Do these sources agree that student protest was focused on Vietnam?*'

Your task is to study them and say how they do or do not agree. In this case, you could say that the cartoon shows there was anti-Vietnam feeling, but does not tell us about student feeling, while Source A clearly shows that at least some students were against the war. The student in Source C shows he's against Vietnam by saying 'I do not have his patriotism for a nation that can't behave decently. I don't believe in the military…'.

Evaluating the utility or reliability of sources

You have to make sure you understand the difference between utility (usefulness) and reliability (accuracy). Remember:

- usefulness is about what you can find out from a source.
- reliability is whether you can believe it.

Let's see how this works with Source A.

In the examination, the sort of question you might be asked is:

'*How useful is this source for a historian studying student feeling about Vietnam?*'

You could say: '*It is very useful because it is talking about students going to Vietnam to see what was happening and coming back and encouraging even more protest about it.*' You also need to address reliability: '*we need to know the author has researched student protest for the book and is trying to give a balanced view*' **and** typicality '*it tells us how some students felt. But this only gives us the views of the protesters, and maybe not all of them. The question says "student feeling" so we would need some evidence about how students who did not go on marches felt about the war*'.

Evaluating a hypothesis

In the examination, the final question will ask you to consider whether the sources support a hypothesis. Obviously, we haven't got the full range of sources here. Let's use one more source.

Source D

A student protest in 1967.

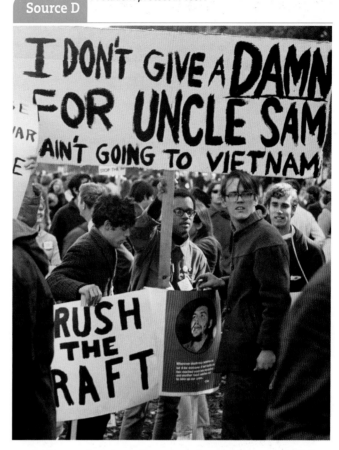

In the examination, the sort of question you might be asked is:

'*Student protest in the 1960s was about nationally significant issues.' How far do the sources on this paper support this view?*'

For this question you need to consider the evidence for and against the statement provided by the sources and also consider the typicality and reliability of the sources. So Source B suggests that Vietnam is a nationally significant issue; it is a cartoon in a national newspaper criticising the war. The written sources suggest that there was a lot of student criticism of the war in Vietnam, as does the photo (Source D). So they do tend to support this view. However, Source C suggests there were other issues – unless he was the only student to feel like this. By the time you do the examination, you will be able to say that your studies have shown you that, while big issues were important, there were also protests about smaller issues at university level, too.

Key Topic 1: McCarthyism and the Red Scare

Although the USA and the Soviet Union (USSR) had been allies during the Second World War, their political differences soon caused problems once the war was over. The Soviet Union was a communist state where a non-democratic government completely controlled the economy. The USA was a democratic country that was capitalist and where the economy was not government-controlled. Both sides wanted the nations of the world to accept their political system. The opposition between them became known as the Cold War.

In this Key Topic you will study:

- the impact of the Cold War
- the development of the Red Scare
- the impact of McCarthyism.

You will see how fear of communism had a significant effect on US foreign policy. People feared that the Cold War could turn into a real war, possibly a widely destructive nuclear war, at any time. At the end of the Second World War, only the West knew how to make the hugely destructive atomic bombs. The US government was desperate to stop the Soviet Union finding out how to make these bombs. You will also see how this fear caused a reaction against communism within the USA, known as the 'Red Scare', which led to people losing their jobs or going to prison because of their political beliefs. Reaction went further – Julius and Ethel Rosenberg were executed after having been convicted of passing nuclear secrets to the Soviets. Soon, the Red Scare was used to persecute other groups such as civil rights campaigners, trade union workers and homosexuals.

The pursuit of communists, real and imaginary, was called 'McCarthyism' after Senator Joseph McCarthy, one of the most active communist hunters. Eventually, McCarthyism declined but even now there are disputes about how real the communist threat was.

The impact of the Cold War

Learning objectives

In this chapter you will learn about:

- the ideological clash behind the Cold War
- how Cold War fear affected US foreign policy
- making inferences from sources.

The **communist** Soviet Union and the **capitalist** West fought on the same side in the Second World War and even made agreements about working together after the war. Once the war was over, many of the countries occupied by the Soviet Union soon had communist governments. The USA watched this spread of communism with growing concern, fearing a communist takeover of Europe that could spread worldwide. President Truman decided to send aid to European countries, suffering badly after the war, to help keep them non-communist.

The Marshall Plan, set up by the US government, gave thousands of millions of dollars in aid to European countries. It provided everything from money, to food, to the railway carriages needed to transport that food. The Soviet Union saw this as an attempt to '**bribe**' these countries into staying capitalist.

Cold War fears drove much US policy, at home and abroad, for many years. People were especially fearful of possible nuclear war, and the USA was desperate to keep the secret of making atomic bombs out of Soviet hands.

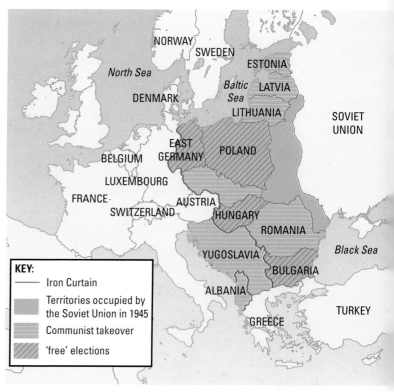

Soviet expansion in Europe by 1950.
Think about which countries might be next.

Source A | Part of a telegram sent to the White House in February 1946 by George Kennan, the US ambassador in Moscow. Think about how this would affect US reactions to the Soviet Union.

The communists believe there can be no permanent co-existence with the US. For Soviet power to be secure, it has to disrupt our society, destroy our way of life and break us as an international power. The Soviets have a highly developed system for working in other countries and they are very experienced and skilful at using it secretly.

Source B | From a speech made by President Truman on 12 March 1947. It outlined the Truman Doctrine – the idea that the USA should help other countries resist communism.

Today, nearly every nation must choose between opposing ways of life. Too often, the choice is forced on them. One way of life, based on the will of the people, has free elections, guarantees of individual freedom, free speech and religion, and freedom from political oppression. The second has the will of a minority forced on the majority. It relies on terror and oppression, a controlled press, fixed elections, and the suppression of individual freedom. I believe the US must support peoples resisting attempted control by armed minorities or by outside pressures. I believe our help should be mainly economic aid to restore economic stability and orderly political processes.

The Berlin Crisis

The first clash of the Cold War was in Berlin. The Soviet Union, Britain, France and the USA all held parts of Germany after the war. The plan was to work together to unite Germany. However, Cold War fears meant disputes broke out, and both sides (the Soviet Union on one side and the remaining countries on the other) made secret plans to exclude each other. Berlin, in Soviet-controlled Germany, was split into four sectors, one for each of the Soviet Union, France, Britain and the USA. The Soviet Union pressed Berliners from all sectors to vote to become communist in 'free' elections. In June 1948, it closed Berlin's transport links out of Soviet-controlled Germany, cutting off supplies into the British, French and American sectors. It looked as if these sectors would be starved into voting communist. So the Western powers flew in supplies, despite the possibility of aircraft being shot down by the Soviets, and dropped them in their sectors. In April 1949, they set up the Federal Republic of West Germany. The Soviets then set up the communist German Democratic Republic. Berlin was split between the two.

Cold War fears hardened. In April 1949, the USA, Canada and Western Europe set up a military alliance called NATO (North Atlantic Treaty Organisation), agreeing to defend each other if attacked. So the Soviet Union set up the Warsaw Pact, a communist version of NATO.

War in Korea

After the Second World War, Korea (like Germany) was occupied by American and Soviet troops and divided into a communist north and a non-communist south. As in Germany, both sides disagreed over unification. They saw Korea as an important symbol in Asia – it mattered whether the united Korea was communist or not. After the war, North Korea elected a communist government; South Korea elected a non-communist one. In 1950, North Korea invaded South Korea and war broke out, with the USA giving military help to the South (acting for the United Nations and supplying troops and a commander) and the Soviet Union supporting the North. The war dragged on until 1954 and ended with the country still divided. The USA began the war saying it would help countries fight communism with aid, advice and supplies. They ended the war prepared to send troops to fight in the name of the USA if another crisis broke out.

Source C The front cover of a magazine sold (and given away free) by a church group in the USA. Think about why they would give it away free.

Results Plus
Top Tip

When asked about the *purpose* of a source, students often concentrate on describing what they see. Students who do well will work out what *message* the author intended to give. For example, Source C was clearly created as a piece of anti-communist propaganda. Churches in the USA saw the Soviet Union as violently opposed to religion. What details tell you that the magazine was trying to create a frightening image of communism?

Source D	From a press conference given by President Eisenhower on 7 April 1954 – Public Papers of the Presidents, 1954.

Question: Mr. President, would you comment on the importance of Indochina [Cambodia, Laos and Vietnam, which had been French colonies] to the free world?

Answer: First, you have the value of a place in terms of its materials that the world needs. Then you have the possibility of many people being taken over by a dictatorship. Finally, you have to consider the 'falling domino' principle. You have a row of dominoes set up, you knock over the first one, and the last one goes over very quickly. Asia has lost 450 million people to the Communist dictatorship; we simply can't afford greater losses. The loss of Indochina could be followed by the loss of Burma, Thailand and Indonesia. That would be millions and millions of people. The possible consequences of the loss are just incalculable to the free world.

Source E	Schoolchildren in the USA in 1951 practising the 'duck and cover' system, supposed to protect them if there was a nuclear attack. These practices were held regularly. Think about what that suggests about how threatened people felt.

Activities

1 Study the map on page 9. In groups, discuss how the map suggests that American fears about the Soviet Union's desire to take over Europe might be reasonable. Think of an argument the Soviet Union could put forward to counter this.

2 In groups, discuss what you can learn from the sources about how Cold War fears affected American policy. Make a table like the one below to show your decisions. Source A has been done for you.

Source	A	B	C	D	E
It suggests...	the American government would become more afraid of communists in the USA				
because...	an important US government official in Moscow told the White House that the Soviet Union would want to destroy the US way of life				

The Red Scare grips the USA

Learning objectives

In this chapter you will learn about:

- the activities of HUAC and spread of the Red Scare
- considering the purpose of a source.

Cold War fears also affected government policy inside the USA. Many people believed the Soviet Union was working secretly inside the USA to overthrow the government and fear of communism grew. The Federal Bureau of Investigation (FBI) built up files on possible communists. The House Committee on Un-American Activities (HUAC), set up by the government, questioned more and more people in a search for Soviet agents. One woman, Elizabeth Bentley, admitted to being a Soviet agent. She gave the FBI names of 150 agents, including 40 government workers. HUAC held more investigations.

HUAC also investigated Hollywood, fearing communists might use the film industry to spread propaganda. Ten Hollywood writers refused to give evidence to HUAC, saying the Constitution gave people a right to free speech and their own political beliefs. Famous film stars, such as Humphrey Bogart, supported the Hollywood Ten, but the Ten were still sent to prison for their refusal to give evidence. The FBI set up loyalty boards to investigate government workers and over 200 were forced to resign. People became less willing to support those investigated by HUAC or the FBI as anti-communist hysteria increased. They did not want to be accused of being communist themselves and face the possibility of imprisonment or losing their jobs or homes.

The Hiss case

In 1948, Alger Hiss, who had advised President Roosevelt and worked for the UN, was accused of being a communist. He had been accused before, but this time HUAC accepted the evidence against him and he was sent to trial. While the trial was going on, the Soviets tested their first atomic bomb, increasing fears of a nuclear war and communist spy rings. The evidence for and against Hiss was complicated and confused. He was found guilty of lying to the court (not spying) and sent to prison for five years. But a guilty verdict meant many people thought he was a spy. He and his supporters still protest his innocence. Information from various Soviet sources after the Cold War ended suggests both his guilt and his innocence.

Source A *Statement issued by the Association of Hollywood Motion Picture Producers, 24 November 1947. Think about why they made this statement.*

Members of the Association of Motion Picture Producers strongly disapprove of the action of the Hollywood Ten. We will sack or suspend, and will not re-employ, any of the Ten until he is acquitted or has given evidence and declares under oath that he is not a Communist.

We will not knowingly employ a Communist or a member of any party wishing to overthrow the US government by force or by illegal or unconstitutional methods. However, we will not be swayed by hysteria or intimidation. We see that there is a danger of hurting innocent people. There is a risk of creating an atmosphere of fear. Creative work cannot be done in an atmosphere of fear.

Source B *From an interview with J. Edgar Hoover, Director of the FBI, in the* US News and World Report, *11 August 1950. Think about why Hoover answered as he did.*

Question: Is the FBI interested in information about any Communists, or only those connected with spy rings or possible **sabotage**?

Answer: The FBI is mainly interested in members of the Communist Party who might be engaged in **espionage**, sabotage, or who are a possible threat to the internal security of the United States. However, the FBI is interested in knowing the identity of all Communists in the United States. Any Communist might be recruited into espionage. He may be handing out peace petitions today. Tomorrow he may be sabotaging American industry or working as a spy.

Despite President Truman's pleas that US citizens had a right not to be punished for their opinions, the House of Representatives passed the McCarran Act to limit the places where communists could be employed and denied them US passports. All communist organisations had to be registered and their members were investigated.

Ordinary people became more and more suspicious of their neighbours. They became less willing to be critical of the government – far less willing to talk politics at all. The problem with HUAC investigations was that the investigation, whether the person was found guilty or not, was a black mark against the investigated person.

13

| Source C | A cartoon from The Washington Post, *24 April 1949. This cartoonist, Herbert Block (who signed himself 'Herblock'), made up the word 'McCarthyism'.* |

"You Read Books, Eh?"

Activities

1 Write a letter to a friend from one of the people who signed Source A. Explain why you signed the letter.

2 Study Source C.

   a Write out the sentence below, using the correct choice between 'approves' and 'does not approve'.

      The cartoonist approves/ does not approve of the investigations.

   b List as many details from the cartoon as you can to support your answer under the following headings

the person being investigated	the evidence the investigators are finding

   c Complete the following sentence, using your examples: *I can tell how the cartoonist feels about the investigations because…*

The impact of McCarthyism

Learning objectives

In this chapter you will learn about:
- how McCarthy played on Cold War fears
- cross-referencing sources.

In October 1949, China became a communist country. This was a big blow to the capitalist West. As anti-communist hysteria increased, Joseph McCarthy, Senator for Wisconsin, made a public speech in which he said: 'I have here in my hand a list of 205 names known to the secretary of state as being members of the Communist Party and who are still working in and shaping policy in the State Department.' The next day, on 10 February 1950, he changed this number to 57. Ten days later, he told the Senate he could name 81. The senate set up the Tydings Committee to investigate his accusations and communist hunting had a new name: McCarthyism.

At first, McCarthy had a lot of support. Twenty-five US states brought in anti-communist laws. The media latched onto his sensational accusations and helped to fuel the hysteria. In many parts of America, anti-communist groups worked to hound suspected people out of their jobs and homes and beat them up. Many of these people belonged to, or had once belonged to, the Communist Party. Levels of fear rose. Now factory workers were also the target of 'red-baiters' (as the communist hunters were known). People in jobs that influenced government policy or how people thought, like teachers or government workers, were targets too.

Source B — From Reds, *a book about McCarthyism written by Ted Morgan in 2003.*

Many newspapers, from Honolulu to Washington, echoed his charges that there was a spy ring in Washington. McCarthyism was catching fire. By March 1950, the donations and the number of letters of support were heavy: 'Why don't you get the rats out of the State Department?'
Drew Pearson [a newspaper reporter later accused of communism by McCarthy] wrote in his diary for 21 March 1950, 'Support for McCarthy seems to be growing. Senator Taft amazed me by admitting that he was encouraging McCarthy.'

Activity

In Source A, McCarthy was said to have had thousands of letters of support.
- Write a sentence explaining why these letters may have been supporting him.
- Write a sentence explaining why these letters may not have been supporting him.

Source A — *A photo used with a newspaper article on 24 March 1950, saying that McCarthy was getting between 5000 and 6000 letters a day supporting his campaign to clear communists out of the State Department. Think about why the photo was taken and what might be in the letters.*

Source C — *Part of an article published in* Time *magazine on 22 October 1951.*

'McCarthyism' is now part of the language. Thousands turn out to hear his speeches. Millions regard him as 'a splendid American' (a fellow senator recently called him that). Other millions think McCarthy a worse menace than the Communist conspiracy against which he professes to fight.

Some have argued that McCarthy's end justifies his methods. This argument seems to assume that lies are required to fight Communist lies. Experience proves, however, that what the anti-Communist fight needs is truth, clearly and carefully presented. As *The New York Times* put it: 'He has been of no use whatever in helping us to find the guilty, but many of us have begun to suspect there must be some good, however small, in anybody who Senator McCarthy opposes.'

Source D — *An 'anti-communist squad' in California attacking suspected communists outside a car factory on 23 July 1950.*

ResultsPlus
Build Better Answers

Exam question: How far do the sources agree about the amount of support that McCarthy had in the early 1950s? (10 marks)

When you are asked about how far sources agree, be careful not to just look for support. Point out lack of support too. To answer the above exam question:

■ **Basic answers (level 1)** suggest the sources agree or not in a generalised way (for example, *they all think he got a lot of support*).

● **Good answers (level 2)** find evidence of agreement or disagreement between sources, giving evidence from them. Answers which show both can get 7 marks. (For example, *Source C says there are millions for him, and the letters in A agree with that. But C also says that there were millions against him*).

▲ **Better answers (level 3)** also consider the extent of agreement, and for full marks will also take into account the reliability or typicality of the sources; (for example, *Source D shows he had some support in factory workers, but that is not all factories, just as senator Taft (mentioned in B) is only one senator (but one who has changed his mind)*).

Activities

1 For each source, write a sentence or two explaining whether you think it shows support for McCarthy and why.

2 Write a paragraph to answer the following question (based on the information you used for the first part of this activity).

How far do the sources support the idea that there was a huge amount of support for McCarthy between 1950 and 1951?

The Rosenberg case

Learning objectives

In this chapter you will learn about:

● the Rosenberg case and its impact

● evaluating the utility or reliability of sources.

On 18 July 1950, Julius and Ethel Rosenberg were arrested as part of an investigation into who passed atomic bomb secrets to the Soviets. The evidence against them, like much of the evidence in communist conspiracy trials, was not clear. It depended a great deal on the evidence of others arrested in the case, including Ethel's brother. It also depended on identifying Julius and Ethel from codenames in Soviet telegrams. The evidence against Ethel was especially weak.

Unfortunately for the Rosenbergs, they were arrested just after war broke out in Korea, a time when fear of communism grew. Many Americans blamed the Rosenbergs for the Soviet Union's ability to make an atom bomb, the invasion of Korea and many other problems in the USA. The Rosenbergs were found guilty and sentenced to death, despite the president's request for Ethel's life to be spared. The spy who gave the Soviets the most useful atom bomb information lived in the UK, where there was less anti-communism. He was sentenced to just 14 years in prison.

Source B	*From the judge's summing up in the Rosenberg case, just before he passed the death sentence on 5 April 1951.*
	Is the language he uses what you would expect from a judge?

Julius and Ethel Rosenberg placed their devotion to their cause [communism] above their own personal safety. They knew they would lose their children, if they were caught. Love for their cause dominated their lives – it was even greater than their love for their children.

The question of punishment comes at a unique point in time. Putting the secrets of the atom bomb into the hands of the Russians has already caused, in my opinion, the Communist aggression in Korea with the resulting casualties exceeding 50,000. Who knows how many millions of people will pay the price of their treason.

Source A	Demonstrators at a New York station on 18 June 1953. They were travelling to Washington to demonstrate in front of the White House. Their aim was to get the president to pardon the Rosenbergs.

Source C — *Written by Dr Harvey Klehr, a professor of politics at a US university, in 1999.*

New evidence shows Julius Rosenberg was a Soviet agent in charge of a spy ring taking scientific secrets, including material about the atom bomb. A telegram from the Soviet Union, seen by the National Security Agency of the USA, describes Ethel as a Communist Party member who knew what her husband was doing.

Source D — *This source is another from a review of* The Secret World of American Communism, *a book written by the author of Source C and some colleagues. The reviewer was not happy with the way Klehr and the other authors had used evidence in their book.*

Not a single document (of the 92 the authors use in *The Secret World of American Communism*) provides evidence of spying. The authors ignore all evidence that contradicts their claim. They make a case by assuming that all evidence of secrecy is evidence of spying.

Source E — *A photograph taken on 15 June 1953. The original caption said: While hundreds of placard-waving demonstrators parade before the White House asking the president to save atom spies Julius and Ethel Rosenberg, they are joined by two pickets with opposite sentiments.*

Source F — *From the website of the National Committee to Reopen the Rosenberg Case. The committee was set up in 1963, and is still at work.*

June 19, 1953 is a never-to-be-forgotten date in American history. On that day, Julius and Ethel Rosenberg died in the electric chair on the frame-up charge of conspiring to commit espionage for the Soviet Union, orphaning their two sons, six-year-old Robby and ten-year-old Michael. Never before in American civil court history had there been an execution for espionage, let alone conspiring to commit espionage. Since then, many Americans have been convicted of spying for the Soviet Union and other countries. Amazingly, some of these spies were FBI and CIA agents. Yet, none have received a death sentence. What made the Rosenberg case unique? The defendants were executed for crimes they were convicted of in the media, but not by a jury in a courtroom. The trial was at the height of McCarthyism and anti-communist hysteria and **paranoia**. For 8 months after their arrest, the Rosenbergs were blamed by the FBI and throughout the media with having caused the United States' undeclared war then raging in South Korea. It was claimed that they did this by having stolen and transmitted the A-bomb secrets to the Soviets. A majority of Americans uncritically accepted these false allegations and clamoured for the harsh punishment of these 'communist traitors'.

ResultsPlus
Top Tip

The language of a source can often show if the source is biased. When asked what a source can be used for, students will do well if they consider the content of the source and also its possible reliability.

Activities

1 In groups, make an index card for each of sources B–F. Say what it is, where it comes from and who produced it. (If it is not possible to answer all these points, write 'can't tell'.)

2 Divide the cards up according to how useful they are in showing the following aspects of the Rosenberg case:

- support for the Rosenbergs' conviction
- opposition to the Rosenbergs' conviction
- the evidence presented in the Rosenberg case
- the importance of the timing of the Rosenberg case.

The fall of McCarthy

Learning objectives

In this chapter you will learn about:

● the fall of McCarthy

● evaluating a hypothesis.

McCarthy promised to prove there were hundreds of communists working for the American government. The Tydings Committee heard his evidence, much of which was very weak. The three Democrat members of the committee signed a statement, on 20 July 1950, that called McCarthy's charges 'a fraud and a hoax, the most wicked campaign of half-truths and untruths in this country's history'. The two Republicans (McCarthy was Republican) refused to sign. McCarthy turned on Senator Tydings and charged him with communist sympathies. He produced more and more accusations, many of them now aimed at his personal and political enemies, including people in the press who had spoken against him. His accusations grew wilder, his evidence more obviously faked. For example, he produced a photo he said showed Tydings with the communist leader Earl Browder. The photo was made from a photo of Browder taken in 1950 and one of Tydings taken in 1938.

In January 1953, the new president, Eisenhower, set up an investigation into communist beliefs among government workers 'to clear the air of unreasoned suspicion that accepts rumour and gossip as evidence'. He gave McCarthy a job on a much less important committee. But McCarthy used this committee to continue his anti-communist campaign. Then he went too far. In September 1953, he began to investigate possible communists in the army. The hearings were on TV and the public saw McCarthy at his worst – bullying army officers such as General Zwicker, a Second World War hero. McCarthy's popularity fell sharply. First the media turned on McCarthy, then the Senate turned on him. On 2 December 1954, the Senate voted to **censure** McCarthy, for improper conduct, by 67 votes to 22. McCarthyism did not instantly die out. Communist-hunting continued, led by HUAC, and the Communist Party was officially banned in 1954 – but McCarthyism was never as wild again.

Source A *From a letter written on 14 January 1954, by Whittaker Chambers, an ex-communist who had testified against Alger Hiss and supported McCarthy. Think about the fact that this is a personal letter not a published report.*

All of us have slowly come to question McCarthy's judgment to some extent. We fear his need to make headlines and his inaccuracies and distortions will lead him, and us, into trouble. It is no exaggeration to say we live in terror that Senator McCarthy will one day make a mistake that will discredit our anti-Communist effort for a long while to come.

Source B *From a television documentary on McCarthy, broadcast on 9 March 1954.*

His main achievement has been to confuse the public between the threat of communism from countries such as the USSR and the threat of communists in the USA. We must not confuse disagreement with communism. We must remember that accusation is not proof. We must not walk in fear of each other. We cannot defend freedom abroad by stopping it at home. McCarthy's actions have alarmed and dismayed our allies abroad, and given considerable comfort to our enemies. And whose fault is that? Not really his. He didn't create this situation of fear; he merely exploited it, rather successfully.

Activities

1 Think about what you have read about the Red Scare.

- Would you say Source B was right that McCarthy did not create the situation of fear?

- How did he exploit it?

2 In groups of three, divide the sources between you. Each person must decide how far the source you have been given supports the statement below. Make sure to list evidence for your opinion from the source.

The Red Scare was just hysteria, that's why McCarthy fell.

3 Hold a debate about the statement above, using the evidence from your source and your own knowledge.

Source C — A Herbert Block cartoon from The Washington Post, *7 May 1954.* Think about why he has called it 'I have here in my hand…'. *(Hint: see page 14.)*

Examination question

What was the purpose of Source C? Use evidence from the cartoon to support your answer. **(8 marks)**

In the Unit 3 examination, you will be required to answer five questions. We are going to look at questions 1 and 2. The examiners think you need about ten minutes to answer each of these questions. So they are not expecting you to write huge amounts. The number of marks helps you judge how much to write. Questions 1 and 2 are based on the chapter in Key Topic 1 called 'The impact of McCarthyism'. In the examination, the sources will be provided in the booklet.

ResultsPlus
Maximise your marks

Question 1

Examiner's tip: question 1 will ask you what you can learn about a particular topic from the sources provided. Be careful not to just copy information from the source. You need to make inferences from the sources – work something out based on the information in them. Let's look at an example (Source C on page 15).

'What can you learn from Source C about attitudes to McCarthy in 1951?' (6 marks)

Student answer	Examiner comment
The source tells me thousands listened to his speeches and millions of people thought he was a splendid American. On the other hand, it also tells me that there were people who thought McCarthyism was worse than communism. The New York Times quote said he was not a help in catching communists.	This answer mainly reproduces information from the source and would get very few marks. Let's rewrite the answer, making inferences and showing how the source helped us make them.
I can learn that <u>many people supported him strongly</u>. **Source C says that huge numbers – 'thousands' – went to listen to his speeches and 'millions' thought he was a splendid American. At least one senator agreed with that. This and the numbers suggest that he had** <u>support from a range of people,</u> **from ordinary Americans to people high up in politics. We can tell that the author of Source C** <u>is against McCarthy</u> **(he describes McCarthy as 'no use' and suggests that he lies to achieve his ends). The fact that even he has to admit that millions of people supported McCarthyism** <u>shows the extent of support for McCarthy.</u> **On the other hand, Source C also shows** <u>that there were people who were against him</u> **and it is clear from Source C's reaction to McCarthy, and the way the New York Times reporter writes, that** <u>opposition to McCarthy was as extreme as support for him</u>.	In this answer there are several inferences made from the source (<u>underlined</u>), using detail from the source to support the deductions (**shown in bold**). This answer would get full marks. It is not the only possible answer – the important thing is to make valid inferences from the source and refer to the source to show how you made those deductions. However, marks are often lost at the end of an examination by spending too much time on the first question. Make sure not to spend more than ten minutes reading, thinking and writing your answer. Three supported inferences are enough to get you full marks.

Question 2

Examiner's tip: question 2 will be a question that asks about the purpose of a particular source. You need to think about the message of the source: what is it trying to say? This is not the same as the purpose of the source, but it helps you think about its purpose: what effect does the person who produced the source want to achieve? You should use your own knowledge of the historical context – what was happening at the time – to help you explain what the author was trying to achieve. Let's look at an example (Source D on page 15).

Study Source D and use your own knowledge. Why do you think a newspaper printed this photo? Use details from the photo and your own knowledge to explain your answer. (8 marks)

Student answer

An anti-communist squad is shown attacking communists. This was during the Red Scare, where some people, especially McCarthy, were saying they were finding communists in government and elsewhere. The newspaper probably wanted to have a dramatic picture, one that showed how violent anti-communism was and how it was affecting ordinary people.

Examiner comment

This answer goes beyond just describing the source in detail. It discusses a valid message for the source. But it does not discuss the purpose – why was the newspaper publishing that photo? Let's rewrite the answer, making the purpose and the message of the photo clear and putting it in context with our own knowledge.

An anti-communist squad is shown attacking communists. This was during the Red Scare, **when people were frightened of the spread of communism in the USA. People like McCarthy were stirring them up and making them think there would be a communist takeover. Some ordinary people took matters into their own hands, like the factory workers in the picture.** The newspaper probably wanted to have a dramatic picture, one that showed how violent anti-communism was and how it was affecting ordinary people. **They probably wanted to discourage people from behaving like this – the anti-communists look like thugs and the communist they outnumber and are beating up looks like a victim.**

Here the message and the purpose of the source are clearly defined and the context is clear.

Key Topic 2: The civil rights movement 1945–62

By 1870, the USA had abolished slavery and given black people equal rights as American citizens. The Fourteenth Amendment to the Constitution (1866) made black people full US citizens. However, black people, especially in the South, still faced racism, segregation, unequal treatment and violence. (Segregation, the policy of separating white and black people, made black people use different, often worse, facilities – such as toilets or cafes – from whites.) Black people were often prevented from voting and, all over the USA, had the worst living conditions and were 'last hired, first fired'. The civil rights movement campaigned more and more widely after the Second World War to stop injustice and inequality.

In this Key Topic, you will study:

- ○ progress, especially in education, and problems in implementation
- ○ the importance of the Montgomery Bus Boycott
- ○ the role of Martin Luther King and further progress and problems 1958–62.

You will see how civil rights protesters tried to stop segregation and other racist policies, using the Supreme Court to overrule racist state laws. Segregation laws were often called Jim Crow laws, after a white singer who did racist impressions of black people. However, the Supreme Court could only overrule state laws if they could prove they were unconstitutional. Even when a federal law was passed, this did not mean that the law was put into practice or accepted in the states whose laws it overruled. Time and again, black people gained legal rights then had to face great danger using those rights. In the case of desegregating schools, where black children went into schools that previously had been only for white children, the risks were taken by children as young as six.

From 1955 to 1962, civil rights leaders such as Martin Luther King attempted to gain civil rights mainly by peaceful, non-violent protest. As the movement grew and gained more and more media attention, opponents of civil rights became increasingly violent to the point of bombing churches full of men, women and children, whose only 'crime' was their colour.

The civil rights movement

Learning objectives

In this chapter you will learn about:

- the aims and diversity of the civil rights movement
- making inferences from sources.

Before the Second World War, organisations such as the National Association for the Advancement of Colored People (NAACP) and the Congress of Racial Equality (CORE) campaigned for black people's civil rights. They fought against **racism**, violence against black people and **segregation**. Under segregation, black people lived in the worst parts of towns and cities and were forced to use separate, usually worse, facilities for everything from education to healthcare. In the North, black people often had the worst living conditions, too.

During the Second World War, over a million black people fought in the US armed forces. Many more worked on the home front. Under pressure from the NAACP, the army appointed more black officers – by the end of the war, there were about 6000 black officers. But the army was not desegregated until 1948, after the war, and then it had to be done by a presidential order.

After the war, black people hoped for more equality and less racism. Some whites changed their attitude to black people after working with them during the war; many more did not. There was still racism, segregation and inequality all over the USA. Southern states still had laws to enforce segregation. They could do this because there are two government systems in the USA. The federal government makes laws that affect all of the USA but each state has the power to make its own laws that can only be overruled by the Supreme Court if they are against the Constitution.

ResultsPlus
Watch out!

Students can get confused about some civil rights terms. *Segregation* is keeping black and white people separate – its supporters are sometimes called separationists. *Integration* is having black and white people living or working together.

Source A	*A poster put up in the South in 1965, attacking Martin Luther King, a civil rights leader. This is actually a picture of King at an integrated (not segregated) leadership training college in Tennessee, not a communist training school. What was the poster aiming to do?*

| Source B | An early NAACP badge. Lynching is when a group of people kill someone they accuse of a crime without a trial. Before the Second World War, about 70 black men and women were lynched each year in the South. After the war there were fewer lynchings. Think about why this might be. |

The impact of the Second World War on black Americans

After the Second World War, more and more black people began to join organisations such as the NAACP or CORE. Others joined more local organisations that campaigned for civil rights, often based in a local church group. Civil rights groups all had the same basic aim: they wanted the rights black people had in real life to be the same as the rights they had legally. A law does not actually give people a right unless it is enforced. However, different groups concentrated on different issues at different times, depending on national and local events. For example, the Montgomery Bus Boycott (which you will study later) targeted segregation on buses in Montgomery, Alabama, because the arrests of two black women for refusing to obey the segregation laws of Alabama brought the situation to a head.

New groups were always forming – some lasted; others did not. All faced opposition from many white people as soon as they had any influence. The Southern Christian Leadership Conference (SCLC) was set up in 1957 after the success of the Montgomery Bus Boycott, underlining the importance of church organisations to the organisation of protests.

One of the big aims of civil rights groups was to get black people registered to vote and then to go to vote in elections. Campaigners knew that politicians would be more likely to help the civil rights movement if there were a large number of black people willing and able to vote for them.

| Source C | From an interview with Claudette Colvin, from Montgomery, Alabama, in 1993. She is talking about her childhood in the late 1940s. She was arrested for not giving up her seat to a white person on a segregated bus. |

When I grew up, the South was segregated. Very much so. Your parents had taught you that you had a place. You knew that much. In the city, you had the signs. You have to stay here, you have to drink out of this [water] fountain, you can't eat at this [lunch] counter. I thought segregation was horrible. My first anger I remember was when I wanted to go to the rodeo [cowboy show]. Daddy bought my sister boots and bought us both cowboy hats. That's as much of the rodeo as we got. The show was at the coliseum, and it was only for white kids. I was nine or ten.

| Source D | From the introduction to a website set up in 1999 by people who took part in the Freedom Movement in the South in the 1960s. |

The media called it the 'civil rights movement,' but most of us who were involved in it prefer the term 'Freedom Movement' because it was about so much more than just civil rights. Today, from what you see in the media and read in textbooks and websites, you would think that the Freedom Movement only existed in a few states of the deep South – but that is not so. The Freedom Movement lived and fought in every state and every city of America: North and South, East and West. There were some differences between the Southern and Northern wings of the Movement, but they were insignificant compared to the Movement's essence. It was the same movement everywhere, fighting for freedom and equality.

Source E

An NAACP demonstration in Houston, Texas, in 1947.
Some of the placards show where they have come from.

ResultsPlus
Build Better Answers

Exam question: What can you learn from Source E about the aims of the civil rights movement? **(6 marks)**

When you are asked what you can learn from a source or sources, you are expected to make *inferences*. This means you work something out about aims from the information in the source.

■ **Basic answers (level 1)** just copy the information (for example, *they wanted freedom*).

● **Good answers (level 2)** make inferences from the sources (for example, *they wanted to fight racism all over the USA*).

▲ **Better answers (level 3)** use details from the sources to support the inferences (for example, *you can see they wanted to fight for equality all over the USA. It shows people with signs against segregation and signs showing they come from all over the country*).

▲ **Excellent answers (full marks)** make three supported inferences.

Activities

1   Read the inferences below that can be made about the aims of the civil rights movement. Copy each inference and write next to it the letter(s) of the source(s) that you think support it. Some sources may support more than one inference.

- To stop violence against black people
- To allow black people to vote
- To end segregation
- To get black people campaigning for their rights

2   Design a poster displaying all the aims of the civil rights movement that you can find in the sources.

Peaceful protest

> ## Learning objectives
>
> In this chapter you will learn about:
> - the tactics, especially non-violent tactics, of the civil rights movement
> - making inferences from sources.

Most early civil rights groups stressed the need for their members to protest peacefully. They took **direct action** – protested in a way that made their protest visible – to get publicity. But, as civil rights leader Martin Luther King said, the publicity should 'leave people in no doubt who were the oppressors and who were the oppressed'. So protestors had to be non-violent. Tactics used by the peaceful protestors included:

- **picketing** – standing outside a place, for example a shop, that discriminated against black people and asking others not to use it
- **boycotts** – not using a service if it discriminated against black people
- **sit-ins** – sitting at segregated lunch counters in shops that would not serve black people
- **freedom rides** – riding on buses to integrate them and using the 'whites-only' toilets and cafes in bus stations
- **mass marches.**

Martin Luther King

Martin Luther King was a **Baptist** minister who became a world famous leader of the civil rights movement. King's first important civil rights campaign was the Montgomery Bus Boycott (see pages 28–29). His Christian faith, and his admiration of the Indian leader Mahatma Gandhi's non-violent protests, meant he was a firm supporter of non-violent direct action. He was an inspiring speaker and convinced many people to take part in demonstrations, boycotts and sit-ins, despite the fact that they were likely to be arrested, imprisoned or attacked by their opponents. He urged his supporters not to be afraid of resisting, 'because what we are doing is within the law'.

Source A *CORE members picketing against shops that would not let black people eat at their lunch counters, 17 May 1960. Think about what made picketing an effective sort of protest.*

Source B *From the CORE website (CORE still exists today). See Source D for an explanation of why CORE organised 'jail-ins'.*

The Congress of Racial Equality (CORE) was founded in 1942 in Chicago. Many of its members were in the Chicago branch of the Fellowship of Reconciliation, a pacifist organisation seeking to change racist attitudes. The founders of CORE were deeply influenced by Mahatma Gandhi's non-violent resistance. In 1942, CORE began protests against segregation in public facilities by organising sit-ins. CORE pioneered non-violent direct action, especially the tactics of sit-ins, jail-ins and freedom rides.

Source C — *From an interview with Martin Luther King in Christian Century Magazine in 1957.*

Privileged groups rarely give up their privileges without strong resistance. So, the basic question confronting the world's oppressed is: How to struggle against the forces of injustice? The alternative to violence is non-violent resistance. The non-violent resister protests by non-cooperation or boycotts, but he does them not for their own sake, but to shame his opponent.

Source D — *Mary King, a civil rights worker all her life, explains the importance of the work of people who, like her, stayed in the office and manned the phones.*

Whenever one of our workers was jailed, or a church mass-meeting was bombed, whenever there was a fire bombing, whenever a local leader's home was shot at, or any other serious incident occurred, Julian Bond [Communications Director of Student Nonviolent Coordinating Committee or SNCC] and I went into high gear. The presence of a reporter at a jail, or even a telephone enquiry from a newspaper, was often the only step that let a local sheriff know he was being watched. Our job, in mobilizing the press, was to make local law officers feel watched, so providing a measure of safety for civil rights workers.

Source E — *Martin Luther King and Ralph Abernathy, civil rights leaders, in prison for protesting against segregation in Birmingham Alabama in 1963. Think about why being jailed might be an effective protest.*

Source F — *From Stride Towards Freedom by Martin Luther King, published in 1958. King is describing what happened on 30 January 1956, after his home was bombed by opponents of the civil rights movement.*

There were hundreds of angry people in front of the house. The police were trying, in their usual rough manner, to clear the streets, but the crowd ignored them. One Negro said to a policeman, who was trying to push him aside: 'I ain't gonna move nowhere. That's the trouble now; you white folks is always pushin' us around. Now you got your .38 and I got mine; so let's battle it out.' I realized many people were armed. Non-violent resistance was on the verge of turning into violence.

I walked onto the porch and asked the crowd to come to order. In less than a moment, there was complete silence. Quietly I told them that I was all right and my wife and baby were all right. 'Now let's not become panicky,' I said. 'If you have weapons, take them home; if you do not have them, please do not try to get them. We cannot solve this through retaliatory violence. We must meet violence with non-violence. Remember the words of Jesus: "He who lives by the sword will perish by the sword."'

Activities

In groups, make a list of all the different kinds of non-violent direct action that the sources tell you about.

Copy and complete the sentence below, using the information in the sources.
Publicity was important to the civil rights movement because...

Read Source C carefully. Write a phrase that would fit on a placard summing up what King is saying.

If you did not have the caption to Source F, you would still know that it was written by a supporter of King. Choose one phrase or sentence in Source F that shows bias towards King and write a sentence to explain your reasoning.

What can you learn from Source E about:

● the tactics of the civil rights movement

● Martin Luther King?

The Montgomery Bus Boycott

Learning objectives

In this chapter, you will learn about:

- the causes, events and results of the Montgomery Bus Boycott
- the role of Martin Luther King
- considering the purpose of a source.

On 1 December 1955, Rosa Parks, a black woman, was riding home from work in the sixth row of seats on a bus in Montgomery, Alabama. Montgomery buses were segregated. The front five rows were for whites only. Black people had to clear any whole row for a white person to sit – even if it emptied the rest of the row. The bus filled up. The driver told Mrs Parks and three other black people to clear a row for a white person. The others moved. Mrs Parks refused, even when the driver threatened her with arrest for breaking the law. The driver stopped the bus and called the police who arrested her.

Rosa Parks' trial was on 5 December. Members of the NAACP (Rosa was also a member) worked with church and college organisations to set up a one-day boycott of Montgomery buses on that day. The court found Rosa guilty and fined her $10. That evening, protesters set up the Montgomery Improvement Association (MIA) to improve integration – beginning with the buses. They chose Martin Luther King as chairman. The MIA asked all black people to boycott Montgomery buses. About 70% of bus users were black, and most black bus users joined the boycott. The MIA planned and organised the boycott very carefully. They organised lifts and asked black taxi firms to charge less during the boycott.

Some employers sacked workers who took part in the boycott. Boycott leaders were arrested (there was a 'no boycott' law in Alabama) and they and their homes were attacked.

The boycott went on for 381 days. It worked because almost every black person carried on supporting it (as did some whites) and because the MIA organised good support for it. The bus company lost a lot of money and Montgomery got a lot of bad publicity, both nationally and worldwide.

Because the state government would not change the law, the Supreme Court had to act. On 19 December 1956, it ruled segregation on buses **unconstitutional** and, as of 21 December, black people rode the bus again. The ruling was unpopular with many white people in Montgomery and elsewhere.

Source A *From a leaflet about the arrest of Rosa Parks, handed out by Jo Ann Robinson, a teacher and head of a group of professional black women in Montgomery. It urged a boycott of buses on the day of her trial. Think about the language she used to get the message across.*

A Negro woman has been arrested and thrown in jail in Montgomery because she refused to get up out of her seat on the bus for a white person to sit down. It is the second time since the Claudette Colvin Case [when, 9 months before, a 15-year-old black girl was arrested in Montgomery] that a Negro woman has been arrested for the same thing. This has to be stopped. The next time it may be you, or your daughter, or your mother. This woman's case comes up on Monday. We are asking every Negro to stay off the buses Monday in protest of the arrest and trial. Please, children and grown-ups, don't ride the bus on Monday.

Source B *Martin Luther King and other members of the MIA ride a bus in Montgomery on 21 December 1956, once the Supreme Court ruling was passed.*

Source C | *In 2001, Colin Bootman, a black artist, painted this image of Rosa Parks being fingerprinted in 1955. Think about why he might choose this subject.*

Source D | *Extracted and paraphrased from a leaflet issued by the Montgomery Improvement Association on 19 December 1956.*

In a few days, the Supreme Court Mandate will reach Montgomery. You will ride <u>integrated</u> buses. This puts a tremendous responsibility on us all to keep, in face of possible unpleasantness, a calm and loving dignity befitting good citizens and members of our Race. If there is violence in word or deed, it must not be our people who commit it.

Now for some specific suggestions:

The bus driver has been told to obey the law. Assume he will help you occupy any vacant seat.

Do not deliberately sit by a white person, unless there is no other seat.

If cursed, do not curse back. If pushed, do not push back. If struck, do not strike back, but show love and goodwill at all times.

In case of an incident, talk as little as possible, and always quietly. Do not get up from your seat! Report all serious incidents to the bus driver.

For the first few days try to ride with a friend in whose non-violence you have confidence. You can help one another with a glance or a prayer.

If another person is harassed, do not go to his defence. Pray for the oppressor and use moral and spiritual force to carry on the struggle for justice.

If you feel you cannot take it, walk for another week or two.

We have confidence in our people. God bless you all.

The Montgomery Improvement Association
The Rev. M. L. King, Jr., President
The Rev. W. J. Powell, Secretary

Examination question

Why might the photographer have taken the photograph in Source B? **(8 marks)**

Activities

1   Who did the author of Source A expect to read her pamphlet?

 ● What does the writer want the readers to do?

 ● Choose one sentence from the pamphlet that you think is aimed at making people act. Copy it out and explain why you chose it.

2   Why might Colin Bootman have painted Source C?

3   Write a note from Rev. Martin Luther King to Rev. Powell giving three reasons why you think you need to publish a leaflet of advice about riding integrated buses. You can infer these from the source. Under the note, make a chart and copy the parts of the source you made the inference from. The first one is done for you.

Reason	Point from source
I. Not to stir up too much trouble from white people.	'Do not deliberately sit by a white person'

Using the law

Learning objectives

In this chapter, you will learn about:
- attempts to obtain civil rights, especially in education, via the constitution
- considering the purpose of a source.

In 1947, President Truman told the Committee on Civil Rights that it was time to make sure civil rights laws were enforced. 'We have been trying to do this for 150 years', he said. However, many state laws enforced segregation and other racist policies. The federal Supreme Court could only change these laws if they could show they were unconstitutional. This should have been easy. The Fourteenth Amendment to the Constitution made black people full American citizens, so any form of discrimination was unconstitutional. But many people in government, especially representatives of Southern states, fought to keep these laws in place. In 1896, in the case of *Plessy v. Ferguson*, the Supreme Court had ruled that facilities, education and transport could be segregated as long as they were 'separate but equal'. The NAACP had brought cases to the Supreme Court for years, in the hope of getting state segregation laws overturned. Mainly because of the *Plessy* case, it was a long, hard struggle, as the example of education shows.

In June 1951, Oliver Brown brought the case of *Brown v. Topeka*, to try to integrate elementary schools in Topeka, Kansas. The case was rejected, because of the *Plessy* 'separate, but equal' ruling. The NAACP urged Brown to try again. They combined his case with four others as *Brown v. the Board of Education*. The other cases were in Washington DC, Delaware, South Carolina and Virginia. On 17 May 1954, the Supreme Court ruled that all school segregation was unconstitutional. However, it did not give a date for integration. A year later, in an extra ruling, it did say this had to be done 'with all deliberate speed' – but there was still no deadline. This left the speed of integration up to individual states, weakening the force of the law.

After the *Brown* case, schools did integrate – some peacefully, some less so. Many states made plans that left integration far in the future. Some white people were very hostile to the idea of integration. White Citizens' Councils were set up in the South to make sure segregation stayed. Within a year, they had spread all over the South.

Source A *From* Collier's, *a magazine that published fiction and articles about issues of the time, 23 February 1952.*

The NAACP has achieved goals that, according to The New York Times, 'would have been impossible ten years ago'. It is carrying out a thoughtfully planned campaign against state laws that support segregation. The NAACP has not the time, money nor desire to help every Negro in trouble. It is mainly interested in cases where constitutional rights are violated, which can be taken to the Supreme Court under the Fourteenth (Equal Rights) Amendment. The NAACP has won 30 of the 32 cases it has taken to the Supreme Court since 1915.

Source B *The head teacher of Glen School, Tennessee, with an integrated class in 1957. Think about who might have wanted this photograph taken and why.*

Source C	From an interview with Linda Brown (one of the black children in the Brown case) in an American documentary filmed in 2004. Think about the possible problems with what she remembers about a famous case after all that time.

We lived in an integrated neighbourhood. I played with children of many nationalities. I remember walking over to Summer school with my dad and going up the steps of the school. And I remember going inside and my Dad talking to someone and then he went inside an office with the principal and I was left sitting outside with the secretary. I could hear voices and they got louder as the conversation went on, and then he came out of the office, took me by the hand and we walked home. And I just couldn't understand what was happening because I was so sure that I was going to go to school with Mona, Guinevere, Wanda and all my playmates.

Source D	From the Supreme Court decision on Brown v. the Board of Education, 17 May 1954.

We conclude that the idea of 'separate but equal' has no place in state education. Separate educational facilities are inherently unequal. Therefore, we hold that the **plaintiffs** [the black people who brought the court case] are, by reason of the segregation complained of, deprived of the equal protection of the laws guaranteed by the Fourteenth Amendment.

Source E	A cartoon published on 17 May 1962, the anniversary of the Supreme Court ruling on Brown v. the Board of Education. The little black girl is explaining that her school is still segregated, despite the ruling. This was true of many schools, all over the USA. Think about the cartoonist's message.

"I'M EIGHT. I WAS BORN ON THE DAY OF THE SUPREME COURT DECISION"

JAMES CROW PUBLIC SCHOOL

HERBLOCK
THE WASHINGTON POST

ResultsPlus
Top Tip

When asked what they can learn from a source, many students just repeat the information in the source, or what they can see in the source. Students who do well will make an *inference*: work out the implications of what the source is saying. So, for Source E, one inference would be that segregation was still widespread enough to be seen as a national issue by the political cartoonist.

Activities

1   In groups, discuss which source you would use to show:
    ● the benefits gained by working for civil rights through the courts
    ● the problems with working through the courts.

2   Write the heading: Factors for progress in gaining civil rights. Then copy out the following points placing them in what you think is their order of importance, with the most important first.
    ● Laws that supported desegregation
    ● Enforcement of laws
    ● Public support for laws to enforce equality.

3   Write a paragraph to explain your choice in question 2.

Integrating Little Rock, 1957

Learning objectives

In this chapter, you will learn about:

- the events at Little Rock
- evaluating a hypothesis

After the *Brown v. the Board of Education* decision, some schools integrated quickly and easily. Others did not. Only two Southern states, Arkansas and Texas, tried to obey the order; the other states refused. Arkansas and Texas did not find integrating schools easy, as the story of integrating Central High School in Little Rock, Arkansas shows.

School officials tried to integrate the school in 1957. They chose nine of 75 black students registered for admission to enter in the first year. The Governor of Arkansas, Orville Faubus, opposed integration. He called out the Arkansas National Guard on the first day of school to 'protect the school' by keeping the black students out. The NAACP had arranged for the students to arrive together, but a mix up meant that Elizabeth Eckford arrived alone. The mob was terrifying, but she managed to reach the soldiers, thinking they would help her get into the school and safety. They turned her back, forcing her to go back through the mob that was shouting '**Lynch** her!' When the eight other students arrived, they were also turned away by the guards and had to face the mob.

There was worldwide publicity. People were shocked, especially by one of the photos (Source D). President Eisenhower felt he had to act. He sent in federal troops to guard the Little Rock Nine. Then he put the Arkansas troops under federal control and had them guard the students. The guardsmen stayed until the end of the school term. The guards had to make sure the students got into and out of the school safely and moved safely between classes. They could not stop white teachers and students ignoring the black students. They did not guard the students' homes and could not stop the hate mail and threatening phone calls.

At the end of the year, the oldest of the Little Rock Nine, Ernest Green, graduated with the rest of his year. There was a seat either side of him at the ceremony because no one would sit next to him. Governor Faubus then closed the school for the next school year, to put off integration yet again.

Source A — Part of an interview with Elizabeth Eckford in 1962.

Most of the white students didn't bother us; they just pretended that we didn't exist. But a small group of white students bothered us every day. They called us names, tripped us up in hallways, and pushed us down stairs without fear of the teachers telling them off. We couldn't fight back; we couldn't even say anything that might provoke confrontation, because then we might be expelled. Every day there was something, our parents too. After the soldiers left, my father came to get me in the car. Often as he walked to the school from the car, he was pelted with rocks. There was a screaming mob outside the school every day.

Source B — From a 1993 interview with Ernest Green, the oldest of the Little Rock Nine.

A small band of students had really raised the level of harassment with Minnie [Minniejean Brown]. I'll never forget this kid. He was like a small dog snapping at Minnie with a steady stream of verbal abuse. He had figured out how many ways he could say 'nigger'. This kid just touched Minnie's last nerve. He was in front of her on the cafeteria line. I was behind her and I could see it coming. Before I could say, 'Minnie, don't do it. Forget him...', she had taken her bowl of chilli and dumped it on his head. The chilli just rolled down his face. The cafeteria help [workers] in Central was black. They all broke into applause. The school board used the incident to suspend Minnie (but not the ones who harassed her), and then finally to expel her. And so coming back from Christmas, we were eight students. It was southern justice. They did what you'd expect them to. In school, some students passed out little cards: 'One down, eight to go'.

Source C	From The civil rights movement, *written by W. T. M. Riches in 1997.*

Despite the sacrifices made by the Little Rock Nine in 1957, it was not until 1960 that Central was integrated. By 1964, only 2.3 per cent of all African American children in illegally segregated Southern states were attending desegregated schools.

Source D	The famous photo of Elizabeth Eckford walking to Central High School on the first day of school. Think about why this photo became so famous.

Activity

In groups, prepare to debate how far the sources support the statement below. Use all the sources in this chapter and also sources A and D (on pages 30 and 31) in the previous chapter 'Using the law'.

By 1957 the civil rights movement had made real progress in integrating schools.

ResultsPlus

Build Better Answers

Exam question: *By 1957 the civil rights movement had made real progress in integrating schools.* How far do the sources support this statement? Use details from Sources A–D and your own knowledge to support your answer. **(16 marks)**

In this question the examiner wants you to look for evidence for and against the statement in the sources and then come to a decision using your own knowledge as well.

■ **Basic answers (level 1)** do not give evidence directly from the sources or from the student's own knowledge.

● **Good answers (level 2)** offer evidence from the sources about support or the lack of it (for example, *they had not made progress. Source C tells us that it was not until 1960 that the school was integrated and A and B tell us the black students had a terrible time*).

▲ **Better answers (level 3)** show that there is evidence for and against the statement, and use all of the sources and own knowledge to come to a decision (for example, they use sources to show the successful legal challenge to segregation, the Little Rock case to show the problems, and decide that the *Brown* decision was still progress).

▲ **Excellent answers (level 4)** additionally consider the overall strength of the evidence (for example, *other schools in Arkansas did integrate more easily but resistance to integration was probably more typical in 1957, since only two of the Southern states tried to obey the order after the Board of Education decision*).

Sit-ins and freedom riders, 1961

> **Learning objectives**
>
> In this chapter you will learn about:
> - sit-ins, freedom rides and violent opposition
> - evaluating the utility or reliability of sources.

Sit-ins

In February 1960, four students organised sit-ins to integrate lunch counters in Greensboro, North Carolina. Sit-ins were not a new form of protest; black people had sat and waited to be served in places that were white-only on many occasions. But the Greensboro sit-ins sparked a wave of similar protests across North Carolina and then the rest of the South. Most of the protesters were students, including students who had travelled from campuses in the North to take part. In March, students in Raleigh, North Carolina, set up the Student Nonviolent Coordinating Committee (SNCC – pronounced 'snick') to organise this growing movement. The SNCC held courses for the protesters, giving them tips about how to remain non-violent in the face of aggression and actual violence.

Freedom riders

In 1961, the Supreme Court passed a law to desegregate the facilities in bus stations. CORE and the SNCC organised 'freedom rides' – buses that would drive through the South 'testing' the facilities in bus stations to make sure they were integrated. They were not expecting this to be the case and they were anticipating a hostile response, especially as they deliberately put white protesters on the buses as well as black ones. The first two buses were attacked and the riders were beaten up at several stops. At Anniston, one of the buses was firebombed. The next week, more buses set off. The riders were imprisoned in Birmingham and beaten up in Montgomery. Over the summer, more than 400 freedom riders were arrested and a much larger number were beaten up. Three were killed, but the freedom riders kept riding.

Source A A professor and two students on a sit-in. All of them had mustard, ketchup and other foods poured over them. The dark stain on Professor Salter's shirt is blood. He was hit repeatedly with a piece of wood. This source shows that different types of people took part in SNCC protests – students and teachers, black and white people.

Source B From a 1993 interview with Gladis Williams, who was a high school student in Montgomery in the 1960s.

> Kress's and H L Green were segregated. By the time we'd get down there usually the police was waiting on us. Let's say a group of six was picketing in front of H L Green, or going to sit in at the counters. The first group would go in, and we'd see what happened to them. If they got arrested, we'd have another group come in. Then they'd get arrested. And all of a sudden everybody would end in jail.

Source C

A photo of the bus that was firebombed at Anniston on 14 May 1961. The 22 riders were able to get out of the bus in time, so no one was killed.

Source D

From a 1970 interview with James Farmer, a black civil rights activist who was on the bus that went into Anniston and was attacked. Think about how an eyewitness source like this might be useful to a historian.

We planned the Freedom Ride with the intention of creating a crisis. We were counting on the racists of the South to do our work for us. We figured the government would have to respond if we created a situation that was headline news all over the world, and affecting the nation's image abroad.

When the bus arrived in Anniston, there was a mob of white men at the bus terminal. They were armed with pistols, guns, blackjacks, clubs, chains, knives – all in plain sight. The Freedom Riders decided not to go into the bus terminal to test the facilities. It would have been suicide. They told the driver and he began to drive on. Before the bus could pull out, members of the mob slashed the tyres. The driver got to the edge of Anniston before the tyres blew and the bus stopped. The mob had followed in cars and surrounded the bus, holding the doors closed. One of them broke a window and threw a firebomb into the bus. There were some local policemen in the mob.

ResultsPlus

Build Better Answers

Exam question: How useful are Sources C and D as evidence of what went on during the freedom rides? **(10 marks)**

■ **Basic answers (level 1)** only give generalised answers, not giving details from the sources or only considering who produced the source (for example, *Source D is useful about the freedom rides because the person was there*).

● **Good answers (level 2)** give details of what the content of the sources is useful for or what we cannot find out from them (for example, *Source D is useful for finding out why people went on freedom rides*), or concentrate only on the reliability of the sources.

▲ **Better answers** combine these elements. They get full marks if they show what the sources are useful for and what they are not useful for and also think about how reliable the source is, bearing in mind who produced it and why. They take into account what difference these things make to how much the sources can contribute to the enquiry.

Activities

1   On an index card write down which source you think best shows the **dangers** faced by civil rights protesters and explain why you chose it.

2   Now do the same for the source you think best shows the **tactics** of civil rights protesters.

3   Now do the same for the source you think best shows the **motives** of civil rights protesters.

Opposition to the civil rights movement

Learning objectives

In this chapter, you will learn about:

- opposition groups, such as the Ku Klux Klan, and their methods
- evaluating the utility or reliability of sources.

There were many kinds of opposition to the aims of the civil rights movement, all over the USA. Southern opposition was the fiercest and the most violent, but there was opposition in the North too. All over the USA, many white people were automatically racist while hardly noticing.

The Ku Klux Klan was the most visible organisation that took violent action – its members dressed in white robes with hoods. The Klan was a 'secret' society, although in many small towns everyone knew who the Klan members were. Other organisations opposed to the civil rights movement included the White Citizens' Council, formed after the *Brown* v. *the Board of Education* decision (see page 30). They protested against integration and also physically attacked black people. When protesters went into Southern states, they knew they could not rely on the people they would usually ask for support. Some judges, soldiers and the police were members of groups like the Klan; there were many more civilians who were simply hostile to integration.

Opposition to integration led many Southern states to defy **federal laws**. In 1962, James Meredith was the first black student to go to the University of Mississippi. There were large-scale student riots on campus that had to be put down by federal troops, leaving many people wounded and two dead. Meredith began classes the next day – with 15,000 soldiers to keep the peace.

Source A — *From the* New York Times, *25 October 1989, referring to a speech made by a member of the Mississippi Sovereignty Commission in 1963. Think about how the person writing the article felt about the speech.*

The speech said that separate drinking fountains and bathrooms were necessary because many blacks lacked morals, education and proper hygiene. 'There are many Negroes, of course, who have reached plateaus of citizenship,' the speech said. 'They are personally clean, have high morals and are educated. However, they are still in the minority.'

The state agency that distributed the speech was the Sovereignty Commission, which, in the 1950s and 1960s, spied on, **infiltrated** and harassed civil rights groups. It also financed the White Citizens' Councils, set up to promote segregation.

Source B — *From a speech by Tom Brady, spokesman for the White Citizens' Council, in response to the* Brown v. Board of Education *ruling in 1954. Brady was a judge in Mississippi.*

Laws cannot kill a sacred custom. When a law conflicts with the wishes of the majority, violence, bloodshed and revolution will follow attempts to enforce it. We are the Southern Negro's friend. We have provided for his needs. Gradually we have opened the door of opportunity to him.

Source C — *From a song sheet printed in Arkansas at the time of the Little Rock Central High School integration, 1957.*

Old Ike* had ordered
To mix the schools
When Mr Faubus said
'Hold it, we are not fools.'

If you know what's good
You'll stop and listen
We're not going to stand for
This Nigger mixing.

Ike called in his troops
To make ready to fight
'Be in Little Rock, Arkansas
Tomorrow night.'

So on came the troops
In numbers bigger and bigger
To make the White folks
Go to school with the Nigger.
(*Ike was a nickname given to President Eisenhower.)

Source D Rioting at the University of Mississippi on the night of 30 September 1962, part of the opposition to integration of the university (by admitting James Meredith, the first black student). The trucks belong to federal troops and the 'smoke' is tear gas, being used to break up the rioters.

ResultsPlus
Build Better Answers

Activities

Think about Source A.

- Write a one-line slogan that carries the message of the speech discussed in Source A.

- Copy one phrase or sentence from the last paragraph that shows Source A itself is probably biased.

- If Source A is biased and the speech it quotes is biased, write a sentence to explain why Source A is still a valuable source.

Which source would you use if you could only use one source to show violent opposition to the civil rights movement. Why would you make this choice?

What aspect of the civil rights movement would you use Source C to show?

Exam question: *Opposition to integration came from all levels of society*.
How far do the sources support this statement? Use details from the sources and your own knowledge. **(16 marks)**
When answering questions that ask you to think about how far your sources support a statement, the best answers consider the nature, origin and purpose of sources as well as the content. If asked to use your own knowledge, make sure you do so.

■ **Basic answers (level 1)** have no support from the sources or own knowledge (for example, *yes, many different sorts of people opposed integration*).

● **Good answers (level 2)** add details from the source (for example, *you have got the judge in Mississippi and the person who wrote the poem – who doesn't seem to be that educated*). This answer could earn more marks if it added a comment on the reliability of the sources.

▲ **Better answers (level 3)** explain how the evidence supports and challenges the statement.

▲ **Excellent answers (level 4)** also consider the extent to which support is provided (for example, *You can find a judge (B) and students (D) and evidence of unthinking prejudice that suggests it is deep in people's thinking (A and C). You have to think that not all judges were in the White Citizens' Council and not all students were against integration (some were civil rights protestors).*

In the Unit 3 examination, you will be required to answer five questions. We are going to look at question 3. The examiners think you need about 15 minutes to answer this question. The number of marks helps you judge how much to write. We are going to focus on the chapter in Key Topic 2 called 'Using the law'.

ResultsPlus
Maximise your marks

Question 3

Examiner's tip: question 3 will ask you if the sources, or a selection of them, support a particular view. You should look for both support and the lack of it, giving specific examples from the sources. You also need to consider the amount of support that the sources do provide. You will get higher marks if you cross-refer between sources, rather than just looking at each source individually. Let's look at an example (using all the sources on pages 30 and 31).
'How far do these sources support the view that integrating schools in the South was a constant battle?' (10 marks)

Student answer	Examiner comment
The sources show that it certainly was a struggle. People in the South did not make integration easy. OR I don't think that they show that. It wasn't a constant battle for all the kids.	These are two different level 1 answers. Level 1 answers decide that the sources either support or do not support the view under discussion and they give a generalised response. Let's see what we would have to do to reach level 2.
The sources show that it certainly was a struggle. People in the South did not make integration easy. In Source E, the cartoonist is saying there still isn't a lot of integration eight years after the Brown v. Board of Education ruling that it had to happen. The little girl is eight years old and she still goes to a Jim Crow School. OR I'm not sure that is true. Source A suggests that there was progress over ten years that was carefully planned to end segregation, which suggests it was working for integration. **It suggests that the battle was being won in some places and so does the classroom photo (Source B) – it shows a nice, peaceful, integrated classroom.**	At level 2, the answers may still argue for support **or** lack of support. However, these answers are better than level 1 answers. They refer to specific sources, and the detail in them, as providing support (or the lack of it) for the statement. The cross-referencing **(shown in bold)** takes the second example nearer to the top of the level. An answer which looked at both support and the lack of it would get 7 marks.

I think some of the sources support it and some of the sources do not. Source B shows an integrated classroom in Tennessee (the South) in 1957. The kids are crowded around the teacher. There are more white kids than black kids, but they are all mixed up. It looks integrated and happily so. Source C suggests a struggle, though. The girl has an integrated life, but the school hasn't caught up and her Dad can't get her into the school her friends are going to. Source E certainly suggests a battle, when taken with Source D especially. Source D is the court ruling that says that separate schools is wrong. Eight years later things still are not sorted out, according to the cartoon.

This is a better answer. It gives evidence from the sources that provide both support and lack of support for the view under discussion and it also cross-refers between sources. But it doesn't yet get full marks. For 10 marks an answer must consider the extent of support shown in the sources, and also consider the nature of the sources themselves. How far are these sources able to support the statement (or not)? Let's see what could make this a full-mark answer.

I think some of the sources support it and some of the sources do not. Source B shows an integrated classroom in Tennessee (the South) in 1957. The kids are crowded around the teacher. There are more white kids than black kids, but they are all mixed up. It looks integrated and happily so, but maybe it was taken especially to show that integration was working. Maybe the school wasn't really like that, or it was the only one in the area. Source C suggests a battle, though. The girl has an integrated life, but the school hasn't caught up and her Dad can't get her into the school her friends are going to. Source E certainly suggests a battle, when taken with Source D especially. Source D says that separate schools is wrong. Eight years later things still are not sorted out, so that looks like a struggle. But Source E is a cartoon where the cartoonist wants to criticise the fact there still isn't a lot of integration and show it as a constant battle to end it.

This is just one example of an excellent answer. Other answers might consider the reliability or typicality of other sources.

Key Topic 3: Changes in the civil rights movement 1963–70

The events of 1961 began a change in the attitude of civil rights campaigners. The violence against freedom riders, including the firebombing at Anniston, was shocking. The lack of federal support for civil rights also discouraged civil rights campaigners. It seemed that the government only acted when they were forced to do so by violence and the publicity that came with it. More and more people began to believe that peaceful protest was not getting anywhere fast enough. Some of them began to support more radical action, including the 'back to Africa' movement, especially as African countries gained independence in the 1960s. Other civil rights campaigners, including Martin Luther King, continued to protest by non-violent direct action.

In this Key Topic, you will study:

- the peace marches in 1963: Washington and Alabama
- Martin Luther King and civil rights legislation
- Malcolm X and Black Power.

You will consider how the growing lack of trust in the government by black people and the escalating levels of violence against them affected the ideas of the civil rights movement, as well as how world reaction to these events affected US government action. You will compare the tactics of civil rights activists, such as Martin Luther King, and those of Malcolm X and Stokely Carmichael.

Changing views

Learning objectives

In this chapter you will learn about:

● how views on segregation changed.

In the 1960s, non-violent protests, and the publicity surrounding them, increased. One of the ways that non-violent direct action was supposed to work was to put pressure on segregationists to change by getting them to show themselves in a bad light in the media. The idea was to shame them into obeying anti-segregation laws. In fact, the pressure produced an increasingly violent reaction. This, in turn, pressured the federal government to act.

During the 1960s, a growing number of black people began to agree with the black Muslims, who argued that integration was too slow in coming and, when it came, did not produce equality. They said black people were discriminated against in integrated schools and workplaces, so they were better off living separately. Other civil rights protestors, such as the Black Panthers and individuals such as Malcolm X (see pages 46 and 47), argued that non-violence was not getting results. They argued that people should defend themselves against violence with violence.

Source A	*Part of a letter written by Martin Luther King while he was in prison in Birmingham, Alabama, in 1963.*

We have waited more than 340 years for our constitutional and God-given rights. Perhaps it is easy for those who have never felt the stinging darts of segregation to say 'Wait'. But when you have seen vicious mobs lynch your mothers and fathers and drown your brothers and sisters; when you have seen hate-filled policemen curse, kick and even kill your black brothers and sisters and go unpunished; when you have to try to explain to your six-year-old daughter why she can't go to the amusement park advertised on television and see a sense of inferiority begin to grow in her; when you drive across the country and have to sleep, night after night, in your car because no motel will take you; when you are humiliated day in and day out by signs that read 'white' and 'colored' – then you will understand why we find it difficult to wait.

Source B	*Black Muslims staging a counter-demonstration at an NAACP rally in Harlem in 1961.*

Activity

The caption does not tell you who Source A was written to. Write a sentence explaining, from the language and tone of the source, what sort of person you think it might be.

Birmingham

Learning objectives

In this chapter you will learn about:
- the events in Birmingham, Alabama
- considering the purpose of a source.

Birmingham, Alabama, had not carried out a single piece of desegregation. It had the nickname 'Bombingham', due to the regular bombings of black houses, churches and businesses. The Reverend Shuttleworth's church organisation, the Alabama Christian Movement for Human Rights, had been working there since 1956. Its chief of police, 'Bull' Connor, was said to have given the Ku Klux Klan 15 minutes to beat up the freedom riders of 1961 before his police moved in to protect them, as the government had ordered. In 1963, civil rights campaigners targeted Birmingham for a full-scale non-violent desegregation campaign.

The campaign began on 3 April. There were anti-segregation marches and Bull Connor's police made many arrests. Among those arrested was Martin Luther King. So many adults were jailed that one of the organisers, James Bevel, began to train children in protest tactics, to make sure that the demonstrations continued. The first big children's demonstration was on 2 May. By the end of the day, 956 children had been arrested. The next day, more children marched. This time, dogs and firehoses were used. The stories and photos of Birmingham were published wordwide. President Kennedy admitted 'I felt ashamed'. By 9 May, some black protesters were breaking down under the pressure, and violence broke out in the poorer part of the city. The mayor and protest leaders met on 10 May to work out how to break down segregation in the city. The next day the governor of Alabama sent in state troops, deliberately disrupting the agreement process. On 12 May, President Kennedy sent in federal troops and calm was restored. The mayor passed desegregation laws and lunch counters and shops desegregated. Black people were able to apply for jobs they had previously been forbidden to apply for. The campaign had worked.

Source A *Part of a letter written by Martin Luther King while he was in prison in Birmingham, Alabama, in 1963.*

In any non-violent campaign, there are four basic steps: collecting facts to see if injustice exists, negotiation, spiritual preparation and direct action. We have gone through all these steps in Birmingham. There can be no denying that racial injustice engulfs this community. Birmingham is probably the most segregated city in the United States. Its ugly record of police brutality is widely known, as is its unjust treatment of Negroes in courts. There have been more unsolved bombings of Negro homes and churches in Birmingham than in any other US city. The purpose of our direct action programme is to create a situation so tense, so full of crisis, that it will force those who refuse to negotiate to do so. We have not made a single gain in civil rights without determined legal and moral pressure.

Source B *From a report in* The National Guardian, *a New York newspaper, for 16 May 1963.*
Do you think the newspaper supported civil rights or not?

We were told the 1000 or so students arrested that day had not been housed or fed. We drove to the jail, the students were in the yard. It began to rain. We got wet, the students got soaked; there was no shelter for them. The cops and their dogs got in the squad car. They stayed dry. That night the weather turned cool. The kids were still in the yard, unfed. People took food and blankets and threw them over the fence.

I was later to see people attacked by dogs and knocked over by firehoses at such pressure that the water stripped bark from the trees and knocked bricks from the walls. The strange thing was, all the brutality I saw in Birmingham was police brutality.

Source C

William Gadsden, who was crossing the road rather than protesting, being set on by one of 'Bull' Connor's police dogs, 3 May 1963. Marches were often held at noon, when people were out over lunchtime. Think about why the photographer took the photo.

Source D

From an interview with Audrey Faye Hendricks in 1993. She was nine years old when she went to jail.

I was in jail seven days. We slept in little rooms with bunk beds. There were about 12 of us in a room. I was in a room with my friends. We called ourselves Freedom Fighters, Freedom Riders. There were only one or two kids in jail who were delinquents [arrested for crimes]. Everybody else was there because of the movement. We ate in a cafeteria. The food wasn't home cooking. I remember some grits [a kind of porridge] and they weren't too good. My parents could not get word to me for seven days. We would get some news, like there was no more room in Juvenile Hall [the jail she was in]. They were taking the rest of the people to the fairgrounds because that was the only place to house them now. The jails were all full.

Activities

1 If Audrey Hendricks (Source D) had been allowed to write a short note home to her parents, what do you think she would have said? Write the note using the source.

2 Read Source B again.
   - Write down three words or phrases from the source that suggest a bias for or against the protesters. Explain your choice.
   - How does the reporter's choice of which aspect of the day to write about reflect that bias?

3 Read Source A again.
   - Why do you think Martin Luther King wrote the letter used in Source A?
   - Give two examples from the letter to show how it helped you to decide why he wrote the letter.

ResultsPlus
Build Better Answers

Exam question: Why do you think Source C was so widely published in the USA and abroad? **(8 marks)**
The following will help you when answering an examination question similar to the one above about the *purpose* of a source.

■ **Basic answers (level 1)** make a general statement, but not refer to the sources or any other knowledge of the context (for example, *because civil rights was a big issue and that made it news*).

● **Good answers (level 2)** also use detail from the source or context (for example, *Birmingham was very anti civil rights, and this shows how bad it was* or *its the kind of photo that tells the civil rights story*).

▲ **Better answers (level 3)** use details to explain the message of the source.

▲ **Excellent answers (full marks)** explain the purpose of publishing the photo, using the source (for example, *the newspaper wanted to show the police behaving badly and a black person, especially a young black man, behaving well. They wanted to get public support for the civil rights movement and opposition to racism*).

The march on Washington

Learning objectives

In this chapter, you will learn about:

- the march on Washington
- evaluating a hypothesis.

The success of the Birmingham campaign led to a wave of civil rights actions all over America. President Kennedy made a speech promising 'to ask Congress to act, to make a commitment it has not fully made in this century to make sure race has no place in American life and law'. But there was still violent opposition to change. Groups such as the Ku Klux Klan carried out bombings and murders, including the killing of NAACP leader Medgar Evers. Black people felt increasingly threatened by the violence and ignored by government. There were riots in many towns and cities. Civil rights groups worked together to organise a march on Washington to convince Congress to act to support civil rights. A Civil Rights Bill was under discussion, but making little progress. The march on Washington was to be the biggest civil rights action ever.

President Kennedy advised against the march, saying it would give those against the Civil Rights Bill a chance to say they wouldn't be forced to vote for it by public pressure. When the leaders refused to cancel, he gave his support to the march, but also tried to control the route and the people who spoke. Estimates of the number of marchers range from 250,000 to 500,000. There were about 3000 reporters and the march was one of the first events to be broadcast live around the world by the newly launched Telstar satellite. The marchers listened to many speakers and singers. Martin Luther King made the last speech, his 'I have a dream' speech, which became instantly famous.

Source A — *Written for* Village Voice, *a New York magazine, in September 1963, by a journalist who travelled from New York to Washington for the march.*

I met a Negro I knew was undecided between Muslim and integrationist policies. I asked him why he had come on the march. He said, 'I came out of respect for what my people are doing, not because I believe it will do any good. I thought it would do some good at the beginning, but when the March started to get approval from "Mastah" Kennedy and they started setting limits on how we had to march, I knew it was going to be a mockery. They were letting the niggers have their day to get all this nonsense out of their system.'

Source B — *From Martin Luther King's speech in Washington on 28 August 1963.*

I have a dream that one day this nation will rise up and live out the true meaning of its creed: 'We hold these truths to be self-evident that all men are created equal.' I have a dream that one day, even the state of Mississippi, a state sweltering with the heat of injustice, sweltering with the heat of oppression, will be transformed into an oasis of freedom and justice. I have a dream that my four little children will one day live in a nation where they will not be judged by the colour of their skin but by the content of their character…

This will be the day when all of God's children will be able to sing with new meaning, 'My country 'tis of thee, sweet land of liberty, of thee I sing. Land where my fathers died, land of the pilgrim's pride, from every mountainside, let freedom ring.'

Source C — *From a book about the civil rights movement written in 1996. (Note: a farce is a joke, a mockery of something.)*

Some members of the movement felt that the march was used by the president to present a prettified image of racial harmony. Malcolm X called it 'Farce on Washington'. Stokely Carmichael of SNCC said it was 'only a cleaned up, middle-class version of the real black movement'.

But the size and diversity of the masses, the emotional intensity of the songs and speeches, and the good humour of everyone under the hot sun, deeply impressed observers. One reporter wrote: 'The sweetness and patience of the crowd may have set a new national standard of mass decency.'

| Source D | From a 1990 interview with Bayard Rustin, a civil rights worker who helped to organise the march on Washington. |

There were about 300 congressmen there, we had invited them to come. They saw how orderly it was, that there was fantastic determination, that there were all kinds of people there, not just black people. They saw there was huge support for the Civil Rights Bill. After the March on Washington, when Kennedy met those who had resisted the bill before the march, he made it clear that he was now prepared to put his weight behind the bill.

Results Plus
Top Tip

When asked whether a source supports a statement, students sometimes forget to refer back to details in the source. Students who do well will give examples from the source and also explain how these support the statement. For example, if answering 'Does Source E support the idea that the march on Washington had widespread support?' a good answer would be: *Yes, because it's a large crowd (this is only part of it) and you can see a mix of age, gender and race. This shows support is not just from one social group.*

45

| Source E | Some of the thousands of people who marched on Washington. Think about the age and colour of the people in this part of the crowd, and the various demands they were making. |

Activity

In two groups, prepare for a debate on the statement:

The march on Washington gave people hope.

Your debaters should use the sources as evidence for their arguments.

Malcolm X

Learning objectives

In this chapter, you will learn about:

- Malcolm X and his message
- evaluating the utility or reliability of sources.

Malcolm X became the voice of many angry black people who felt non-violent direct action had failed. He had had a troubled childhood and joined the Nation of Islam while in prison. The Nation of Islam was a black group that shared many Muslim beliefs. They also believed that attempts at integration had failed and that black people would be better off living separately (even returning to Africa) rather than in an integrated society where they always had the worst living and working conditions. Many black Muslims replaced their surnames (often that of the slave owner who had owned their ancestors) with the letter X, to represent their lost African name. Malcolm X was a member of the Nation of Islam until 1964, when he left following many angry disagreements with its leader.

Malcolm X spoke out against non-violent action and criticised leaders such as Martin Luther King. He had different priorities. Martin Luther King wanted to work with white politicians and convince them to work for civil rights; Malcolm X did not. He saw white politicians as the enemy, and his speeches made that very clear. While Martin Luther King focused on voter registration and desegregation in the South, Malcolm X focused on the inequalities faced by black people everywhere, North and South. While he assured people he was not urging violent revolt, he did urge meeting violence with violence.

Source A A bookstore in Harlem, New York, photographed in 1964. Black people could register for the Back to Africa movement here. Think about what its owners might mean by 'proper propaganda'.

Source B From a speech made by Malcolm X on 3 April 1964 in Cleveland, Ohio.

It's time for you and me to be more politically mature, to realise what the **ballot** [vote] is for. If we don't get to cast a ballot, then we're going to have to cast a bullet. It's either a ballot or the bullet. In the South, you don't get a ballot. In the North, they do it a different way. When Negroes begin to get too much political say in an area, the white man changes the district lines. I haven't seen a Negro change any lines, they don't let him get near the line. No, the white man changes the situation. And usually it's the white man who grins at you most, pats you on the back and is supposed to be your friend. He may be friendly, but he is not your friend. What I'm trying to tell you is this: you and I are not facing a segregationist conspiracy, we're facing a government conspiracy. The government that you go abroad to fight and die for is the government that is conspiring to deprive you of your voting rights, your economic opportunities, decent housing, a decent education. It is not just your employers; it is the government of America that is responsible for the oppression and exploitation of black people in this country.

Source C *From a speech made by Malcolm X on 31 December 1964 to a group of black students from Mississippi who had come to New York to visit various civil rights groups.*

How do you think I feel – I belong a generation ahead of you – to have to tell you 'we sat around like a block of wood while the whole world fought for human rights, so now you still have that same fight'? We did nothing. Don't you make the same mistake. You'll get your freedom by letting your enemy know you'll do anything to get it. Don't you run around trying to make friends with somebody who's depriving you of your rights. They're not your friends, no, they are your enemies. Treat them like that and fight them and you'll get your freedom.

Source D *From* Look Out Whitey! Black Power's Gonna Get Your Momma! *a book about Black Power (see page 54) written in 1968. Think about why the author chose that title.*

More than anyone else, Malcolm X was responsible for the growing awareness and militancy among black people. His clear words cut the chains on black minds like a giant blowtorch. He didn't want to wake America's conscience about black rights. He knew America had no conscience.

Source E *The only meeting between Malcolm X and Martin Luther King, in Washington, on 26 March 1964. How might this photo be misinterpreted without the caption?*

Activities

1   Write a sentence to explain how you could you use Source E and the caption information to show:

   ● unity between Martin Luther King and Malcolm X

   ● lack of unity between Martin Luther King and Malcolm X.

2   Design a banner that gets across the message in Source B in a short phrase.

3   How useful is Source B in showing the views of Malcolm X on what black people needed to do to get their rights?

4   Copy out two sentences from Source B, Source C or both that you would use if you wanted to show that Malcolm X was encouraging black people to violence.

ResultsPlus
Build Better Answers

Some questions ask you to consider the *utility* of a source.

■   **Basic answers (level 1)** give a comment on usefulness, but do not provide detailed support.

●   **Good answers (level 2)** consider what the source is for and its limitations.

▲   **Excellent answers (level 3)** consider the usefulness of the source, its limitations and how its nature, origin and purpose affect what it can contribute to the specific enquiry.

President Kennedy and civil rights

> ## Learning objectives
>
> In this chapter you will learn about:
> - influences on Kennedy to promote civil rights
> - cross-referencing sources.

Various American presidents had tried to enforce civil rights laws. They wanted the support of black voters, but needed the support of senators and voters from the Southern states, many of whom opposed civil rights laws. As a result, laws were watered down, or only enforced in crises, making no one happy. In 1960 Senator John F. Kennedy was standing for president. It was Kennedy who pressed for King's release in October 1960, after which King's father remarked: 'I've got a suitcase full of votes, my whole church will vote for Kennedy.' Kennedy won the presidential election of November 1960 with 75% of all black votes.

Once Kennedy became president, black people hoped he would push through effective civil rights laws and enforce them. But while Kennedy clearly admired Martin Luther King and was convinced by his arguments, he also wanted to keep the Senate happy. He was less forceful than they had hoped. Kennedy gave some key government jobs to black people and set up committees to work out how to improve education, housing and work opportunities for black people. He made speeches supporting civil rights. Martin Luther King, and other civil rights leaders, kept urging Kennedy to act decisively.

Kennedy was driven to act by the rising levels of violence, especially by the worldwide publicity of events in Birmingham in 1963 (see page 42). He had meetings with various African leaders at the White House in 1963. He wanted an alliance with these black leaders. Violence against black people in his own country was an embarrassment to him. In June 1963, Kennedy committed himself to getting a new Civil Rights Bill passed and enforced. The march on Washington showed how much public support there was for this bill among many different groups in America. It also showed strong opposition to it. Two weeks after the march, four young black girls were killed when a church in Birmingham was bombed.

Source A

Kennedy with the United States Commission on Civil Rights on 22 November 1961. He asked for a complete report on progress in civil rights in the last century. Think about what this would actually achieve for black people. How many of his commissioners are black?

Source B | From The Civil Rights Movement, *written by W. T. M. Riches in 1997.*

Civil rights campaigners were increasingly frustrated at Kennedy's lack of action, especially his failure to desegregate government funded housing, something he promised to do 'at the stroke of a pen' during his election campaign. Eventually, in November 1962, he signed an executive order to desegregate [housing], but with no system to enforce it.

Source C | From President Kennedy's television speech in June 1963, *after events in Birmingham shocked the world. No president had ever spoken about civil rights so directly. Think about the impact his speech would have.*

Today, we are committed to a worldwide struggle to help and protect the rights of all who wish to be free.

Difficulties over segregation and discrimination exist in every city, in every state, producing in many cities a rising tide of discontent that threatens public safety.

We preach freedom around the world, and we mean it. But are we to say to the world, and much more importantly to each other, that this is a land of the free except for Negroes?

Source D | From The Civil Rights Movement, *written by Steven Kasher in 1996. The Civil Rights Bill said that a sixth grade education was needed to register to vote; it is the same as finishing primary school in the UK.*

SNCC leaders came to feel that the Kennedy administration's support of voting rights was always going to be betrayed by its refusal to anger Southern authorities. SNCC saw the weaknesses of the bill. In his March on Washington speech, the SNCC leader, John Lewis, summarised their new goal: 'The voting section of this bill will not help thousands of black people who want to vote. It will not help the citizens of Mississippi, Alabama and Georgia who do not have a sixth grade education. "One man, one vote" is the cry in Africa. It must be our cry, too.'

Source E | A cartoon printed in a Chicago newspaper on 5 June 1963.

RUNAWAY

 ResultsPlus
Top Tip

When considering whether a set of sources supports a statement, students who do well will look for evidence *for* and *against* the statement. For example, in the final question in the Activity box below, the key thing to consider is whether Kennedy made important advances in civil rights and whether there is evidence of disappointment with his achievements.

Activities

1 What can you learn from Source C about Kennedy's reasons for drafting the Civil Rights Bill?

2 Write a paragraph explaining whether Source D agrees with Source B's assessment of the Kennedy administration's action on civil rights.

3 *President Kennedy achieved important advances in civil rights.*

   In groups, complete a table like the one below to respond to this statement, using all the sources.

Source	Evidence for the statement	Evidence against the statement
A		

Freedom Summer

Learning objectives

In this chapter, you will learn about:

• the events of Freedom Summer

• making inferences from sources.

Mississippi was the most racist and segregated state in the United States, with a population that was 45% black. However, very few black people voted in Mississippi. They were threatened, attacked, even beaten to death, to stop them voting. The literacy tests a person had to pass to register to vote were used to stop black people voting. Segregation meant that most black people had a poor education in inadequately funded schools. Those who read well were given difficult passages to read, or were simply told they had not passed.

The SNCC had been trying to raise black voter registration in Mississippi for years. They decided on a new strategy for 1964. They selected mostly white northern college students from good families as their volunteers. These students could pay their way and any violence against them would be more newsworthy because of their class and colour. About 1000 students volunteered to go to train people to pass voter registration and to set up community projects such as Freedom Schools, which taught black history as well as subjects such as maths.

The first volunteers left on 20 June. CORE workers Michael Schwerner and James Chaney drove a group to the town of Meridian. The next morning, they heard a nearby black church, chosen as a Freedom School, had been burned down. Schwerner, Chaney and another worker, Andrew Goodman, went to investigate and were arrested. The deputy sheriff released them in the middle of the night, knowing a mob was waiting. Their bodies were found on 4 August. They had all been shot in the head. Chaney had been beaten first – many of his bones were shattered.

At least six civil rights workers were killed in Mississippi during the summer. There were 80 beatings, 35 shooting 'incidents' and over 1000 arrests. Over 60 black homes, businesses and churches were bombed. About 17,000 black people tried to register to vote that summer; only about 1600 succeeded. But the campaign did help to focus attention on black voting rights.

Source A
Students on their training course before setting off for Mississippi.
Why do you think they are singing and holding hands?

Examination question

How useful are Source B and Source D in showing the effects of Freedom Summer?

(10 marks)

Source B
From an interview with Thelma Eubanks in 1993. Thelma was 15 years old during the Freedom Summer of 1964. She became a civil rights campaigner.

We were introduced to black authors who we didn't know anything about at the time. Richard Wright and James Baldwin. I thought they were good. I also remember Freedom Road by Howard Fast and Strange Fruit by Lillian Smith. We hadn't had any of that at school. All we had was Harriet Tubman and the Underground Railroad, Eli Whitney and the cotton gin, and George Washington Carver and the peanut. I guess it was the first time I really heard black success stories. And the Freedom School was the first time I had a social relationship with whites. It just made me know that everyone in the world wasn't like the Southerners.

| **Source C** | *From an interview with Euvester Simpson in 1993. She was born in Mississippi and worked for SNCC from the time she left high school, including during Freedom Summer.* |

I think being involved was probably the most important thing I've ever done in my whole life. It taught me first of all that black people could come together, and we could organise, and we could make some things happen for ourselves and for other people as well. I knew that was where I was supposed to be, and it was just so right. I wouldn't trade it for anything in the world, even though we lost some people along the way.

| **Source D** | *Poster issued by the Federal Bureau of Investigation on 29 June 1964, eight days after the civil rights workers were arrested.* |

MISSING CALL FBI

THE FBI IS SEEKING INFORMATION CONCERNING THE DISAPPEARANCE AT PHILADELPHIA, MISSISSIPPI, OF THESE THREE INDIVIDUALS ON JUNE 21, 1964. EXTENSIVE INVESTIGATION IS BEING CONDUCTED TO LOCATE GOODMAN, CHANEY, AND SCHWERNER, WHO ARE DESCRIBED AS FOLLOWS:

ANDREW GOODMAN   **JAMES EARL CHANEY**   **MICHAEL HENRY SCHWERNER**

	ANDREW GOODMAN	JAMES EARL CHANEY	MICHAEL HENRY SCHWERNER
RACE:	White	Negro	White
SEX:	Male	Male	Male
DOB:	November 23, 1943	May 30, 1943	November 6, 1939
POB:	New York City	Meridian, Mississippi	New York City
AGE:	20 years	21 years	24 years
HEIGHT:	5'10"	5'7"	5'9" to 5'10"
WEIGHT:	150 pounds	135 to 140 pounds	170 to 180 pounds
HAIR:	Dark brown; wavy	Black	Brown
EYES:	Brown	Brown	Light blue
TEETH:		Good: none missing	
SCARS AND MARKS:		1 inch cut scar 2 inches above left ear.	Pock mark center of forehead, slight scar on bridge of nose, appendectomy scar, broken leg scar.

SHOULD YOU HAVE OR IN THE FUTURE RECEIVE ANY INFORMATION CONCERNING THE WHEREABOUTS OF THESE INDIVIDUALS, YOU ARE REQUESTED TO NOTIFY ME OR THE NEAREST OFFICE OF THE FBI. TELEPHONE NUMBER IS LISTED BELOW.

DIRECTOR
FEDERAL BUREAU OF INVESTIGATION
UNITED STATES DEPARTMENT OF JUSTICE
WASHINGTON, D. C. 20535
TELEPHONE, NATIONAL 8-7117

June 29, 1964

Results Plus
Top Tip

When they are asked what can be learned from a source students who do well will make *inferences* rather than simply repeat information. Inferences you can make from Source B include *that she learned to be proud of black authors and black culture and also that her school did not present children with examples of black success.*

Activities

1 Choose the adjective below you think best describes the people in Source A. Write a sentence to explain your choice.

   young   idealistic   united   determined

2 In groups, use the main text and Source D to work out how James Chaney was treated differently from Goodman and Schwerner by their murderers. Decide why you think this was and what this tells you about the killers.

3 Write a paragraph for a newspaper reporting on one aspect of the Freedom Summer campaign. Write about one of the subjects below. Use the sources for evidence.

- The kind of person who worked for the Freedom Summer campaign
- The benefits of the campaign
- The dangers of the campaign

Landmark laws

> ### Learning objectives
>
> In this chapter, you will learn about:
> - the Civil Rights Act of 1964
> - the Voter Rights Act of 1965
> - cross-referencing sources.

Source A

President Johnson shaking hands with Martin Luther King after signing the Civil Rights Act in 1964. Why do you think he asked King to go to the signing?

Civil Rights Act

On 2 July 1964, the new Civil Rights Act was passed. President Johnson pushed the act through against Southern opposition because of the high level of interest in civil rights set off by media coverage of Freedom Summer in Mississippi, in both the USA and other parts of the world. The act banned discrimination in education, public places and work, and set up an Equal Opportunities Commission to investigate discrimination. It made discriminatory state laws illegal. It said that voter registration tests should be the same for black and white people.

The act stopped Southern states giving black people harder passages to read than whites, but there was nothing to enforce this. Laws only work if they are enforced. Black people needed to have federal help in having a fair test for registration and in being protected from violence. Of the five million possible black voters in the South, only two million were registered to vote. In Mississippi, only 6.4% of possible black voters were registered, even after Freedom Summer. So civil rights groups decided to have another push for voter registration, beginning in Alabama, at Selma, where there had been violent clashes when black people tried to register to vote.

On 7 March 1965, civil rights marchers going from Selma to Montgomery were stopped by state troops at the Edmund Pettus Bridge. The troops fired tear gas and attacked the marchers with clubs and electric cattle prods. Mounted troops moved in, attacking the marchers and then attacking anyone on the streets in the part of the city black people lived in. Once again, the USA made world headlines for its abuse of black people. President Johnson provided a federal troop escort so the marchers could finish their march to Montgomery and made a speech in which he said 'all of us must overcome the crippling legacy of **bigotry** and injustice'.

The Voting Rights Act

On 6 August 1965, the Voting Rights Act set a national literacy test for voting – an education equivalent to UK Year 6. It also set up federal examiners who could go to any state and check black people were not being discriminated against in voter registration. This stopped states from imposing their own literacy rules or other rules, such as saying that voters must have their own property to be registered to vote.

Source B *From a speech given by Martin Luther King at the start of the voter registration campaign in Alabama in 1965.*

At the rate they are letting us register it will take 103 years to register all 15,000 Negroes in Dallas County who are qualified to vote. Our cry to Alabama is simple: give us the ballot. We are not begging for the ballot. We are demanding the ballot.

Source D *People registering to vote in Alabama in 1966. These people are registering at their local shop. Several Southern states had to use local shops and halls as well as their own building to register black voters in 1966 because there were so many wanting to register.*

Source C *From* The Civil Rights Movement, *written by W. T. M. Riches in 1997.*

Julian Bond of SNCC commented in 1968 that, 'The '64 and '65 Acts took the pressure off the country. People weren't as concerned about civil rights because they felt they'd done what they should.' President Johnson wrote in his memoirs: 'With the passing of these Acts the barriers to freedom began tumbling down. At long last the legal rights of American citizens – the right to vote, to have a job, to use public places, to go to school – were given solid protection.'

Examination question

How far do the sources agree about the success of the Civil Rights Act and the Voter Registration Act?

(10 marks)

ResultsPlus
Top Tip

When asked about the usefulness of sources, students sometimes assume that they can simply say the same thing about all sources of the same type, for example that eyewitness evidence is always useful. Students who do well will also think about the how *typical* or *reliable* the source is.

Activities

1 In pairs, discuss the views of Julian Bond and President Johnson about the impact of the Civil Rights Act and the Voter Registration Act. Do you think they would agree that the Acts needed to be passed?

2 Do these sources support the view that the Civil Rights Act and the Voter Registration Act were victories for the civil rights movement? Make a table like the one below, to analyse the sources.

Source	Supports because	Does not support because

Black Power

Learning objectives

In this chapter, you will learn about:
- some aims and tactics of Black Power groups
- making inferences from sources.

The Voting Rights Act meant more black people registered to vote. But, especially in the South, it was hard for them to find a party to vote for that supported civil rights rather than opposing it. In 1965, Stokely Carmichael and other SNCC workers in Lowndes County, Alabama, set up a political party, the Lowndes County Freedom Organisation, which focused on black rights. The party symbol was a black panther and the party slogan was 'Vote for the panther, then go home'. The aim was to get black people to actually go out and vote, rather than just staying at home. Many people did, although not enough to get a party member elected.

Black people still faced discrimination and violence and felt, often rightly, they could not trust the government or the police to protect them – much of the violence against civil rights campaigners came from the police. In June 1966, James Meredith (the first black student at the University of Mississippi in 1962) led a March Against Fear through Mississippi. He was shot on the second day of the march. Martin Luther King took over the march, joined by Stokely Carmichael of SNCC. King's speeches stressed the need to continue non-violent action, but the more **militant** speeches of Stokely Carmichael, urging people to demand 'Black Power', gained increasing support.

The Black Panthers

In October 1966, in Oakland, California, Huey Newton and Bobby Seale set up the Black Panther Party. The group had a ten-point plan, but the one that the media paid most attention to was the monitoring of police brutality and carrying guns for self-defence (which was legal in California, as long as guns were not concealed). The Panthers had a uniform: black jackets and trousers, blue shirts and a black beret. Many black people came to see them as a more effective community police than the state police force. They also organised community projects, such as free breakfasts and healthcare in poor black areas. Not surprisingly, the government saw them as a threat, especially as the movement spread. By 1968, there were Black Panther groups in 25 American cities.

Source A *From a 1990 interview with David Dawley, a white civil rights campaigner in the 1960s.*

Willie Ricks from the SNCC asked people what they wanted; they answered, 'Freedom Now'. He urged them not to demand 'Freedom Now' but 'Black Power'. And he kept on and on until everyone was roaring 'Black Power'. It was chilling. Suddenly, I felt threatened. It seemed a message to well-meaning Northern boys like me, 'Go home, white boy, we don't need you'. Later, around the tents, there was hostility. To many people I wasn't David anymore. I was a 'honkey'. We left the march a couple of days later. When we came, we had felt wanted. When we left, we didn't feel wanted. There was a sense that this was the time for black people to lead the strategy and whites should not be involved. We accepted that.

Source B *A Black Panther badge from the 1960s. The phrase 'Power to the People' was picked up and used by many other protest groups. Why do you think this was?*

Source C *From a 1990 interview with Arlie Schart, a SNCC worker who was on the March Against Fear.*

Stokely gave this really fierce speech, in which he said we couldn't count on support from the white man and that blacks had to do it on their own. He said blacks were being sent to Vietnam and killed when they couldn't even vote. They had no rights in their own communities and were going to have to gather the courage to do it on their own. Many people saw this as a cry for separation – but many black leaders, even if they supported the idea of Black Power, still wanted integration. They saw it as the only way to get justice all through the USA.

Source D *From a book about the civil rights movement written in 1990. Think about the message behind the image of a black panther.*

The explosion of black consciousness in Lowndes County, Alabama, had a national, and international, impact. The image of the black panther – the snarling black cat ready and able to defend itself – spread through Alabama and was adopted by the Black Panther Party in California. By the end of the 1960s the image was being used in most major US cities and even in Europe.

Source E *A simplified, shortened version of the Black Panthers' ten-point plan of 1966, based on a full version on the Black Panthers' website. Point 1 was suggesting a form of separation, but with government funding.*

1   We want freedom. We want the power to run our black and oppressed communities.
2   We want full employment for our people.
3   We want an end to the capitalist exploitation of our black and oppressed communities.
4   We want decent housing, fit for human beings.
5   We want a decent education for our people, that teaches us our true history and our role in the present-day society.
6   We want completely free healthcare for all black and oppressed people.
7   We want an immediate end to police brutality and murder of black people, other people of colour, and all oppressed people inside the US.
8   We want an immediate end to all wars of aggression.
9   We want freedom for all black and oppressed people now held in US federal, state, county, city and military prisons and jails. We want trials by a jury of peers for all persons charged with so-called crimes under the laws of this country.
10 We want land, bread, housing, education, clothing, justice, peace and people's community control of modern technology.

Source F *A Black Panther poster from 1970. What is there about the words and the picture that a government might find threatening?*

Activities

1   Read Source E.
    ● Write a sentence saying what you think is the most *radical* aim and explaining why.
    ● Write a sentence saying which aim you think would be most *disturbing* to the US government and explaining why.
    ● Write a sentence saying what you think is the most *surprising* aim and explaining why.

2   In groups, discuss the ways in which the aims of the civil rights movement were different from those of the Black Panthers. Decide on three points of similarity and three points of difference in their aims.

Riots

> ## Learning objectives
>
> In this chapter, you will learn about:
> - riots in cities, 1965–68
> - considering the purpose of a source.

From 1965 on, waves of riots swept the USA. Mostly in towns and cities in the North, they were often set off by a particular act of police brutality, which is why different cities had riots in different years. However, the riots were a reaction to more than police brutality. They were a reaction to the long-term problems of city-living for black people – unemployment, overcrowding and poor services. In 1967, Martin Luther King said of the riots: 'Everyone underestimated the amount of rage the Negroes were feeling but holding back and the amount of prejudice that white people were hiding.'

There were major riots in New York (1964), Los Angeles (1965), Chicago and Cleveland (1966), Newark and Detroit (1967) and Washington and Cleveland (1968). There were smaller riots in other towns and cities. There were hundreds of deaths, thousands of arrests and billions of dollars' worth of damage. Non-violent actions also fell apart into riots, such as a march for union rights in Memphis, Tennessee, led by Martin Luther King in 1968.

On 4 April 1968, Martin Luther King, standing on the balcony of a motel in Memphis, was assassinated by a white gunman. The violence that followed was worst in Washington and Cleveland, but there were riots in over a hundred American towns and cities over the week that followed. It took over 55,000 soldiers to stop the riots. The riots caused $45 million worth of damage and 46 people (41 of them black) died. Thousands were injured and 27,000 were arrested. Many white people who had previously supported the civil rights movement turned against it. The image of innocent, non-violent black people being persecuted by white police was replaced in their minds with the image of an angry black young man with a petrol bomb.

Source A	Jerry Farber remembered his experience of the night of 15 August in Los Angeles in an article written in 1969.

By the next night, Thursday, the people of Watts were in possession of a good part of their own community. A carload of people from the Non-Violent Action Committee went down. This time we didn't take any whites. We'd taken five the night before and they had barely made it out. There were police barricades around the 'riot perimeter', as they called it. We had to park the car and sneak in in twos and threes. We saw a crowd emptying a small grocery shop. They threw bottles to break the street lights, but there was no fighting. Once, two kids began to square up to each other, but someone said 'save it for whitey, brother' and they stopped.

Source B	From a report about the night of 15 August 1965 in Los Angeles, written by a black reporter for the Los Angeles Times, 16 August 1965. Think about the language used in this source and in Source A.

Negros raced cars through the deserted streets of Los Angeles, throwing petrol bombs into shop after shop and shouting a slogan from a radio DJ: 'Burn, baby, burn!' Streets crowded with rioters on Thursday night were wrecked but empty tonight. It was almost like a ghost town. Speeding cars criss-crossed the area. Occupants exchanged the now familiar finger salutes (one for a group from the Watts area, two for the Compton area, three for the Willowbrook area) and shouted 'Burn, baby, burn!' A large part of Los Angeles was burning now, and anyone who didn't return the password was in danger. I learned to shout it too, after being shot at several times. Shops were burning, many had been looted. I only saw two undamaged businesses in the riot zone. Both were petrol stations, one operated by black people, one by white people.

Source C *A still image from a TV news report of the riots in Los Angeles in August 1965. It shows the Watts area of the city. How might people watching TV at the time react to these images?*

ResultsPlus

Top Tip

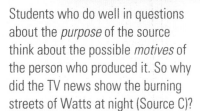

Students who do well in questions about the *purpose* of the source think about the possible *motives* of the person who produced it. So why did the TV news show the burning streets of Watts at night (Source C)? Was it:

- to use a dramatic image
- to show what was happening as it happened
- to scare people
- for another reason?

Activities

1 Read Sources A and B. Work in pairs.

Often, the words people use to describe a situation tell you how they feel about that situation. Copy the table below and fill it out, giving the message which is conveyed by the words in the first column.

Word/phrase	Feeling conveyed
'riot perimeter' (Source A)	*Putting it in inverted commas shows it is not a term the writer agrees with*
in possession of a good part of their own community (Source A)	
emptying a small grocery shop (Source A)	
looted (Source B)	
anyone who didn't return the password was in danger (Source B)	

2 Does Source A support Source B's account of that Thursday night in Los Angeles?

The assassination of Martin Luther King

> ### Learning objectives
>
> In this chapter, you will learn about:
> - King's assassination
> - King's place in the civil rights movement
> - cross-referencing sources.

During the 1960s, several important American political figures were assassinated. President Kennedy (November 1963) was followed by Malcolm X (February 1965) and Martin Luther King (April 1968). King was assassinated on 4 April while in Memphis, where he had gone to support a strike of refuse collectors.

Just four weeks after the assassination, Ralph Abernathy, one of the leaders who took over from King, set out from Memphis to lead a group of marchers to Washington. They were going to continue the Poor People's Campaign, which King had organised. The aim of the campaign was to set up a camp near the Lincoln Memorial in Washington in order to make the poor visible to the nation's most powerful politicians. Resurrection City, as the camp became known, remained in place for about two months. It rained almost continuously and the atmosphere was not one of unity and hope but one of disorganisation and despair. People fought among themselves and the National Guard eventually broke the camp up with tear gas attacks.

Various civil rights groups poured money into keeping Resurrection City running, only to find that far fewer people were now willing to give money to support the movement. This was not just because of the death of Martin Luther King, although he had been an excellent fundraiser. It was as much about the changing image of black civil rights – the increasing violence, the increasing unwillingness to accept help from whites. Groups were less able to stage big demonstrations and civil rights became just one issue of many that the US government had to face. The biggest of these was growing protest about the war in Vietnam (see pages 64–69).

Source A | *From a 1990 interview with Ralph Abenathy, who had worked with Martin Luther King since the 1955 Montgomery Bus Boycott.*

I heard what sounded like a firecracker. And I jumped and turned and could only see his feet outside on the balcony. And I rushed to his side and knelt there patting his cheek and saying 'Martin, Martin, don't be afraid. This is Ralph, this is Ralph.' And I got his attention and he calmed down. Andrew Young came up the stairs and said, 'Oh God. Oh God, Ralph, it's over.' And I got very angry and said, 'Don't you say that, Andy. Don't you say that. It is not over.'

Source B | *From a 1990 interview with Harry Belafonte, a black entertainer and civil rights campaigner.*

I talked with Coretta King [Martin Luther King's wife] and we talked about going to Memphis and being there – meeting the garbage workers, carrying on the campaign, even before Dr King was buried. Everyone in the family agreed it was the right thing to do. It was important that the country knew that, even in our grief, we were still committed to the aims of the movement and that the fall of Dr King didn't mean the movement had lost its courage or its vision.

Source C | A poster from a collection in the US Library of Congress, used between 1968 and 1980. What does it tell you about black voter registration between those dates?

somebody paid the price for your right

register/vote

A. Philip Randolph Educational Fund

Source D | From the New York Times Magazine, 26 May 1968. What is the reporter suggesting about feelings towards the government inside the civil rights movement?

Dr King today would be as much a captive of the times as Ralph Abernathy is. It may not strike certain whites (or Negroes) as right when Abernathy puts on African prayer beads, not a clerical collar, and talks with the black militants with loaded guns. But Dr King was moving in the same direction. He was killed just as he had made peace with Stokely Carmichael and had issued his most forceful challenge to the federal government and whites generally. Many Negroes believe the CIA assassinated Malcolm X just as he was beginning to talk of working with King. They wonder if Dr King was killed by the same people for the same reason.

Results**Plus**

Build Better Answers

Exam question: *The death of Martin Luther King was the end of hope for the civil rights movement.*
How far do the sources support this statement?
Explain your answer using the sources and your own knowledge.

(16 marks)

This question asks you to look for evidence for and against the view and to come to a conclusion. The best answers consider the nature, origin and purpose of the sources as well as their context.

⬤ **Good answers (level 2)** give specific examples which support or challenge the statement (for example showing that Sources A and E both show a continuing campaign).

▲ **Better answers (level 3)** give evidence of both support and challenge to the statement.

▲ **Excellent answers (level 4)** also evaluate the evidence in coming to a conclusion about the extent of support.

Activity

In groups, choose a spokesperson and prepare notes for a debate on the following statement: *The death of Martin Luther King was the end of hope for the civil rights movement.*

Use evidence from the sources and your own knowledge to support your view. Make notes of evidence that supports your view AND evidence that can be used against your view.

In the Unit 3 examination, you will be required to answer five questions. We are going to look at question 4. The examiners think you need about 15 minutes to answer this question. The number of marks helps you judge how much to write. We are going to focus on the chapter in Key Topic 3 called 'Malcolm X'.

Results Plus
Maximise your marks

Question 4

Examiner's tip: question 4 will ask you how useful selected sources are as evidence for a particular query or enquiry. You need to focus your answer on the usefulness of the sources for that enquiry not their usefulness in general. Let's look at an example (Source B on page 46 and Source D on page 47).

'How useful are Sources B and D as evidence of Malcolm X's view of white politicians? Explain your answer.' (10 marks)

Student answer	Examiners comments
Source B is useful. Malcolm X said it.	This is a poor level 1 answer. It only considers one of the sources and gives a very general answer to the question. The answer is considering where the source has come from, rather than how useful it is. Let's see what you would need to do to reach level 2.
The sources both tell us that Malcolm X doesn't trust white politicians. In Source B he says, 'we're facing a government conspiracy'. In Source D, the author doesn't talk about politicians particularly, but is implying it in, 'America had no conscience'. OR Source D doesn't mention white politicians at all. So I don't think you could use it for that. It is more about the effect Malcolm X had on people.	These are two different level 2 responses. At level 2, the answers take information from the sources to show how useful (or not) the student thinks the sources are. Better answers deal with both sources.

In Source B, Malcolm X is making it clear how he feels about white politicians: 'the white man changes the situation'; 'he is not your friend'; 'we're facing a government conspiracy'. Source D is harder to work out. The writer doesn't talk about white politicians as such. But he does make it clear that Malcolm X didn't trust a lot of people – 'America' probably means most white Americans. I'd rather use Source B though; it is more clearly useful about white politicians in particular.

This answer is good enough for 7 marks. It is looking carefully at the usefulness of the content of both sources, and thinking about the limitations of source D.

In Source B, Malcolm X is making it clear how he feels about white politicians: 'the white man changes the situation'; 'he is not your friend'; 'we're facing a government conspiracy'. **The problem is, this is just part of one of his speeches. He might have been being particularly hard on white politicians in that speech, in that place. But he's so forceful about it, you would think it wasn't a message he could change about and it's Malcolm X's own words, so I would say it was very useful.** Source D is harder to work out. The writer doesn't talk about white politicians as such. But he does make it clear that Malcolm X didn't trust a lot of people – 'America' probably means most white Americans. **You'd think, from the way Source D is written, that the author would be biased in Malcolm X's favour and would give a particular view of him that Malcolm X would have approved of. We know the author was a civil rights campaigner and wrote a lot of books about black issues.** I'd rather use Source B though, it is more clearly useful about white politicians in particular.

To get full marks on this type of question, an answer also needs to include a clear consideration of how reliable or typical the sources are. The answer must refer to the sources to explain its views on reliability/typicality and must then relate this to how useful the source is. Note the bold passages where the answer does this.

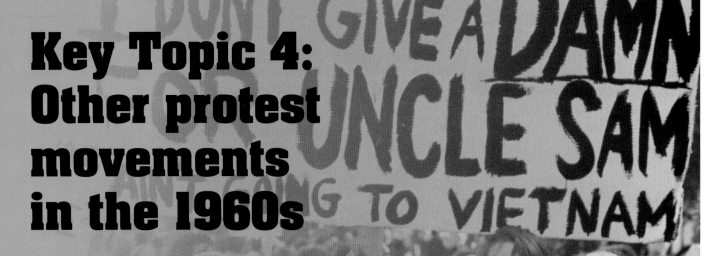

Key Topic 4: Other protest movements in the 1960s

The 1960s were a time of protest – especially among students and other young people. This happened across Europe, not just in the USA. For the first time, large numbers of young people were rejecting the values of older generations. Some 'dropped out' of 'normal' life and set up a new counter-culture with its own values and social organisation. Many more experimented with parts of this counter-culture and protested about the issues that mattered to them, including the war in Vietnam and the rights of women. The 1960s were later called the 'swinging' 60s, referring both to the way that youth culture swung away from their parents' culture and to the greater sexual freedom young people had.

In this Key Topic you will study how these movements developed in the USA including:

- the reasons for student protest
- key features of the student movement
- the women's movement.

You will see how the student movement grew and became more radical, and the effect it had on American society. You will also see how the women's movement also became more radical in its activities and its demands, and how this set off fierce opposition.

The USA in the 1960s

Learning objectives

In this chapter, you will learn about:

● how the USA changed after the Second World War

The American economy had done well after the war. Many people found their standard of living rose – they bought homes, cars and consumer goods such as TVs. More young people went away to study at universities. John F. Kennedy was elected president in January 1961, a symbol of the new, young, successful age of America. He promised a fairer, more equal society.

However, there was another side to the story. We have seen that black people suffered inequality in terms of their rights and their standard of living. Poor white families, especially in rural areas, went through hard times too. Women who had been encouraged to work during the war were expected to go back to running the home, whether they wanted to or not. Kennedy introduced some social reforms to help the poor. After his assassination in 1963, the new president, President Johnson, pushed through laws to raise the minimum wage and improve housing.

The Cold War created fears in various parts of the world about possible nuclear war with the Soviet Union. The Cuban Missile Crisis brought war so close that the US secretary of defence said: 'I thought I'd never live to see another Saturday night.' The war that dominated the USA in the 1960s, though, was the anti-communist war in Vietnam. The US government could call up men as young as 17 years to fight in Vietnam for two years. Those same young men were not seen as responsible enough to vote until they were 21.

Source A | *From a US government website that gives a brief history of each decade of American history.*

Many Americans feared the end of the Second World War might bring hard times. Instead, consumer demand fuelled strong economic growth. New industries such as electronics grew rapidly. A housing boom added to the expansion. The nation's GNP rose from about $200,000 million in 1940 to $300,000 million in 1950 and to over $500,000 million in 1960. At the same time, the rise in births following the war, known as the 'baby boom', increased the number of consumers. More and more Americans joined the middle class.

Source B | *Media and advertising after the war were full of images of the woman as a wife and mother, with a spotless home. The 'perfect' family was white, middle-class with a working father, a housewife mother and two children – a boy and a girl. The husband and wife shown here, Lucille Ball and Desi Arnaz, were married in the TV show they starred in and in real life.*

Activities

1 Write a paragraph, in the style of Source A, to show the downside of life in the USA after the war. Use the information in the main text.

2 Lucille and Desi, from Source B, ran a film studio and made television shows. Both worked, and Lucille had little time to be a housewife. Why do you think they are shown as they are on the magazine cover?

'Turn on, tune in, drop out'

Learning objectives

In this chapter you will learn about:

- reasons for student protest in the 1960s
- making inferences from sources.

The numbers of students grew in the 1960s. Some students became dissatisfied with American society and wanted to see change. The attitude of this significant minority to their parents' generation was summed up by the badges some of them wore, warning: 'Don't trust anyone over 30.'

One important activist group was Students for a Democratic Society (SDS), set up in 1960. It organised sit-ins and other protests over issues ranging from student involvement in university decision making to the war in Vietnam. At first, protests were peaceful, using the non-violent methods of the civil rights movement. When this had little effect, some talked of violent revolution.

Some students protested by refusing to live by normal social rules, setting up a counter-culture with its own rules, often summed up by a phrase first used by one of its leaders, Timothy Leary, in 1968: 'turn on, tune in, drop out'. One of the most influential 'drop-out' movements was the hippie movement, which horrified the older generation by its emphasis on peace, free love, communal living and the use of drugs such as LSD.

What did students protest about? There were almost as many reasons as there were students. They protested against the way universities were run – their rules for students and the fact they 'processed' students to fit their parents' society. They protested against injustice and social inequality. They protested against the 'rat race' of society, where you had to conform to traditional rules to succeed. They protested against war, especially the war in Vietnam.

Source A — *Student enrolment in American universities, 1947–70, from official statistics.*

Year	All students	Women (per cent)
1947	2,338,226	29%
1950	2,281,298	32%
1955	2,653,034	35%
1960	4,145,065	38%
1965	5,920,864	39%
1970	8,580,887	41%

Source B — *Part of the* Port Huron Statement, *outlining the aims of the SDS and drawn up in 1962.*

When we were kids, the US was the richest, strongest country in the world. Freedom and equality for everyone, government of, by, and for the people – these American values were good principles to live by. As we grew up, we saw the problems. The declaration 'all men are created equal...' rang hollow in the face of Negro life in the South and the Northern cities. The Cold War, symbolized by the Bomb, made us aware that we, our friends and millions of others, might die at any time.

We seek a democracy where each person can take part in making decisions about his life and that of his community. Love, reason and creativity should hold power, not privilege, wealth and birth.

In the last few years, thousands of American students have campaigned against racial injustice, war and violations of individual rights. They brought debate back to university campuses after the inaction of the McCarthy period. They also gained concessions, especially in the fight against racism.

ResultsPlus
Top Tip

When a question asks what you can learn from a source, students who do well think about what the source is implying, as well as the information. For example, in Source C, the phrases, 'Don't stand in the hallway, Don't block the hall' and 'Please get out of the new one if you can't lend a hand' are telling the older generation that they should help the younger generation to run things their way, or get out of the way.

Source C	From the protest song The Times They are a Changin', written in 1963 by the protest singer Bob Dylan. What is the message sent to the government and parents?

Come senators, congressmen
Please heed the call
Don't stand in the doorway
Don't block up the hall
For he that gets hurt
Will be he who has stalled
There's a battle outside
And it is ragin'.
It'll soon shake your windows
And rattle your walls
For the times they are a-changin'.

Come mothers and fathers
Throughout the land
And don't criticize
What you can't understand
Your sons and your daughters
Are beyond your command
Your old road is
Rapidly ageing.
Please get out of the new one
If you can't lend your hand
For the times they are a-changin'.

Source D	A student, interviewed in 1970.

I reject everything my father stands for.
I do not want to gear my life to making
money. I do not want to get ahead. I do
not have his patriotism for a nation that
can't behave decently. I don't believe in the
military, the Republican Party or the First
National Bank.
I believe in the brotherhood of nations
and working at a job that reaches you as
a human being. I believe in love and I
believe that we can have a better society
than the one we have now. I believe that
a man ought to read, listen to music and
think. Above all, a man ought to be able
to do his own thing. If he wants to wear
long hair, or a beard, or dress in unusual
clothing, he should be encouraged, not
just allowed, to do so.

Source E	A cartoon published in the Washington Post on 1 August 1967. The man is President Johnson, who became very unpopular over the Vietnam War, because many people felt the money should be spent helping the poor in the USA instead. Do you think the cartoonist approved of the Vietnam War?

"THERE'S MONEY ENOUGH TO SUPPORT BOTH OF YOU ----
NOW, DOESN'T THAT MAKE YOU FEEL BETTER?"

Activities

1 In pairs, make a list of all the reasons for student protest that you can find in the sources (writing the source letter next to the reason).

2 Design a poster or write a ten-line song giving all these reasons.

How did students protest?

Learning objectives

In this chapter you will learn about:

- types of student protest
- the increase in violence by protesters and police
- cross-referencing sources.

Different ways to protest

Students in the 1960s used many of the protest methods used by the civil rights movement. Many student activists joined civil rights campaigns too. Student activists held demonstrations, sit-ins and marches. They broke the laws they saw as wrong – in the same way as civil rights protestors broke segregation laws. But student protest did have particular types of protest. For example, young men often sent back or burned their draft cards (used by the government to call them up to fight in Vietnam for two years) to protest against the war in Vietnam.

As the 1960s progressed, student protests became more organised, more large scale and more violent. Protestors were caught in a growing spiral of violence with the police. The student protest movement had a big impact because the students involved were mainly middle class, educated and white. Their protest did have an effect on government actions (especially in Vietnam), despite the fact that they represented a minority of students.

Key features of student protest

Most student campus protests in the 1960s had the following key features.

- The protest was begun by a small group – often the most radical students.
- Protests lasted several days.
- They often targeted several issues pulling in students for many different reasons.
- Protesters used the tactics of disruption learned in civil rights protests: sit-ins, occupations, strikes, getting arrested.
- The campus authorities called in the police; there were arrests.
- Throughout the 1960s, the protests got larger and more violent, as did the police response.

Source A — *From an interview with Rennie Davis for a US television documentary in November 1996. Davis was a protest leader in the 1960s, working for SDS.*

I would say most people were non-violent. In the large protests that I helped to organise, all were committed to non-violence. People did feel we should be more aggressive as the war kept on and on. It came down to: are we going to abandon non-violence, are we going to take up guns, what are we going to do? And we got bogged down in the arguments. Then King and the Kennedys were assassinated. There were riots all over the country and all the incidents with the riot police.

We went to Chicago intending to pull back in the face of police with billy clubs, to not fight. Chicago was life threatening, it really was. We chanted, 'The whole world is watching,' because demonstrators were being clubbed by police and so were the reporters from TV networks. The police pulled people who lived next to the park off their porches and beat them senseless.

Source B — *How protest changed 1964–70.*

Berkeley 1964	sit-ins marches passive resistance
Columbia 1968	more people involved: sit-ins marches occupations of buildings
Kent State 1970	more people involved: sit-ins marches occupations of buildings destruction of papers burning buildings

Source C — From America Divided: the Civil War of the 1960s, *written by Maurice Isserman and Michael Kazinin, 2000.*

Some SDS members, like Tom Hayden, went to Hanoi [Vietnam] and came back praising 'the fearlessness, calm determination and pride' shown by Vietnamese revolutionaries confronting the world's greatest superpower. Viet Cong flags began to appear in anti-war demonstrations and marchers chanted slogans like 'Ho, Ho, Ho Chi Min, the NLF [Vietnam rebels] are gonna win!' SDS publications filled with images of guerrillas waving guns. The dangers of the politics of confrontation were clear to some, but they were powerless to stop it. Lee Webb, an SDS member, wrote in 1965: 'Calls to stand in front of a troop train, burn a draft card have replaced analysing and understanding the situation.' But it was hard to argue with success. It was militant action, not debate, which increased membership of the SDS. By the end of 1967, it had about 30,000 members.

Source D — Anti-Vietnam demonstrators in Washington in 1967. 'Uncle Sam' was the USA. The photo on the red placard is of the Cuban leader Fidel Castro. The USA and USSR had nearly gone to war in 1962 over Castro letting the USSR base nuclear missiles in Cuba.

Examination question

How far do Sources A, B and D agree about the level of violence in student protest in the 1960s? **(10 marks)**

Activities

1 Copy the table on page 66.
- underline the types of demonstration that you know were also used in civil rights demonstrations
- circle the types of demonstration also mentioned in Source C.
2 Write a paragraph to explain how far Sources A, C and D agree about violence at student demonstrations.

The Kent State shootings

> **Learning objectives**
>
> In this chapter, you will learn about:
> - the events and impact of the shootings at Kent State
> - evaluating the utility or reliability of sources.

On 4 May 1970, National Guardsmen shot four unarmed students during a campus protest against the Vietnam War. The shooting came on the fourth day of increasing violence on campus. Demonstrations began because President Nixon, despite having promised to withdraw troops from Vietnam, had instead sent troops into neighbouring Cambodia and Laos to fight North Vietnamese there. A number of students on campus had already served in Vietnam. On Friday 1 May, a group of students met to bury a copy of the Constitution. They felt Nixon's decision ignored the Constitution – it was dead so should be buried. A student decided to bury his discharge papers too (that proved he had served his two years in the army). That evening, there was trouble in the university town and the police closed the bars. This just put angry people out on the streets. Fights broke out, property was damaged and there were arrests.

The following evening the campus Officer Training Corps building was burned down – there was a lot of resentment that the military had a training camp on campus. Over the weekend, there were various demonstrations. The National Guard had been called in. At times, relations between the Guardsmen and the protesters were friendly, but some demonstrators insulted the soldiers and tried to provoke them to violence. On Monday 4 May, about 2000 protesters gathered for a meeting, which the National Guard tried to break up, mostly using tear gas. A state of emergency was declared because the commanders felt the National Guard was no longer in charge of the crowd. Evidence about what happened next is confused, but about 12.30 pm Guardsmen fired on the protesters, killing four of them and seriously wounding nine.

Source A — From an article written about the Kent State shootings in 1998 by Jerry M. Lewis and Thomas R. Hensley from the Sociology Department of Kent State University.

In the nearly three decades since 4 May 1970, many books have been written analyzing the events. Despite this, there is still much misinformation and misunderstanding about the events of 4 May. For example, a well-known college-level US history book by Mary Beth Norton (also used in high schools) summarises the events: 'In May 1970, at Kent State University in Ohio, National Guardsmen confronted student anti-war protestors with tear gas. Soon after, with no provocation, soldiers opened fire into a group of fleeing students. Four young people were killed, shot in the back, including two women who had been walking to class.' Unfortunately, this short description contains four factual errors: (1) there was some provocation to the Guard; (2) the students were not fleeing when the Guard opened fire; (3) only one of the four students who died, William Schroeder, was shot in the back; and (4) one female student, Sandy Schreuer, was walking to class, but the other female, Allison Krause, was part of the demonstration. This article tries to deal with the historical inaccuracies that surround the May 4th shootings by a resource that teachers can turn to for teaching or student research tasks.

Source B — From Kent State, a book about the shootings written by James Michener in 1971.

At 12.22 the guards left the fence, where they had suffered much humiliation. [Students had also thrown bricks, taken from a construction site, Michener says]. At 12.24, some guardsmen on the right suddenly stopped and swung almost right around and took aim with their rifles. Three students from the School of Journalism had tape recorders running and the recordings agree about what happened next. There was a single shot (some people heard it as two shots at almost the same time), then a silence of about two seconds. Then about eight seconds of gunfire, another silence and two final shots.

Activities

1 Write a paragraph explaining whether Sources A and B agree.

2 In pairs:

- make a list of at least three reasons why information about the shootings at Kent State might be confused
- make a list of where you might get eyewitness information about the shootings and what might affect the reliability of this evidence.

3 In pairs, decide which source you would use to show what happened at Kent State and be ready to explain why.
Write a sentence or two about what you might have thought Source C showed if you did not have the caption.
In what way do Source D and Source E on page 47 tell you similar things about the importance of captions?

Source C *This photo was taken just after the student, Jeffrey Miller, was shot dead. The girl kneeling beside him is Mary Ann Vecchio. She was not a student but a fourteen-year-old who had run away from Miami. She did not know Miller. The photograph won the student photographer, John Filo, a national prize and was published all over the world. Always find out as much about an image as you can by reading the caption carefully. Think about how a lack of information might make you make wrong guesses about an image.*

The position of women in the early 1960s

Learning objectives

In this chapter you will learn about:

- views of the role of women in the 1950s and early 1960s
- position of women in the workforce
- making inferences from sources.

In the 1950s and early 1960s, most people expected women to be homemakers. The general feeling was that single young women could work while waiting to 'catch' a husband and leave work to start a family. But that was all. Many people did not want to employ women in 'career' jobs (with more responsibility and better pay). They argued that women, no matter how capable, didn't need careers – work was a temporary thing. Women's organisations, such as the Federation of Business and Professional Women (set up in the 1920s), were largely ignored. Even people fighting other forms of prejudice (such as racial prejudice) often had a prejudiced view of women. Female civil rights campaigners, and women in other radical groups, were expected to do the secretarial work, not lead or make speeches.

Some people fought the idea that women were just homemakers. Eleanor Roosevelt, the wife of Franklin D. Roosevelt (president from 1933 to 1945), campaigned for equality for women before the war. During the war, she pressed for childcare for women working on the home front. At first, people listened to Eleanor because she was Roosevelt's wife. But she was so popular by the time he died that she was urged to run as vice president. She refused, but continued to campaign for women's rights until her death in 1962. Just one year later, *The Feminine Mystique*, by Betty Friedan was published. Friedan asked the women she had graduated with in 1942 about their lives, what they were doing and if they were happy with their circumstances. Most of the women were either housewives or in low-paid jobs and felt unhappy about their lives. So she interviewed younger women too, and found the same thing. The book was a bestseller and changed the way a lot of people thought about the role of women.

Source A — *From an article about Eleanor Roosevelt on a US government website.*

During the Second World War, Eleanor Roosevelt encouraged women's employment in the defence industries. She urged women to volunteer for civil defence work and the military. She defended women in the military who wanted to do more than type, file, and clean. She campaigned for legislation to set up on-site day care for defence workers. Her insistence that President Kennedy appoint more women to his administration led him to create a Presidential Commission on the Status of Women and appoint Eleanor Roosevelt as its chair.

Source B — *From* The Feminine Mystique, *written by Betty Friedan in 1963.*

The problem lay buried, unspoken, for many years in the minds of American women. Each wife struggled with it alone. As she made the beds, shopped for groceries, matched furnishing fabric, ate peanut butter sandwiches with her children, drove them to Cub Scouts and Brownies, lay beside her husband at night – she was afraid to ask even of herself: 'Is this all?'

There was no word of this feeling in all the novels, and books and articles by experts telling women their role was to seek fulfilment as wives and mothers. They learned that truly feminine women do not want careers, higher education, political rights – the independence and opportunities that old-fashioned feminists fought for.

Source C | *This is an advertisement for a fridge from the 1960s. Think about how it shows a woman's role.*

Source E | *From a document about the role of women in the SNCC, presented to the SNCC anonymously in November 1964.*

The average SNCC worker finds it difficult to discuss the woman problem because of the assumptions of male superiority. Assumptions of male superiority are as widespread and deep-rooted and every much as crippling to the woman as the assumptions of white supremacy are to the Negro. Consider why, in SNCC, women who are competent, qualified, and experienced, are automatically given the 'female' jobs such as typing, telephone work, filing, library work, cooking, and the assistant kind of administrative work but rarely the 'executive' kind.

Source D | *Information from the US Bureau of Statistics.*

Census information for 1960 shows that:
- 38% of students at university were women
- 38% of women went out to work.

Of women working:
- 98% worked in other people's homes
- 68% did clerical work, such as filing and typing
- 14% were managers.

Examination question

What can you learn from Source C about the position of women in the 1960s?

(6 marks)

Activities

1. Using Source A, copy and complete the following sentence:
   Eleanor Roosevelt pushed for women's rights by...

2. In pairs, make a list of at least three features of a woman's role in the early 1960s shown in Source C.

3. Write a sentence explaining why the behaviour of the men in SNCC [Source E] might be seen as surprising.

4. Draw up a table to show the evidence provided by the sources about views of the role of women in the early 1960s, using the headings:
   - Source
   - View of women's role
   - Evidence.

5. Write a paragraph explaining how Sources A and B are useful to a historian studying the role of women in the 1960s.

Women's liberation movements

72

Learning objectives

In this chapter, you will learn about:

- groups that campaigned for women's liberation
- cross-referencing sources.

In 1963, the Equal Pay Act made it illegal to pay women less for doing the same job as men. But it did not abolish discrimination and was unclear about how 'same job' was defined. The 1964 Civil Rights Act made it illegal for employers to discriminate on sexual grounds, as well as religious and racial ones. But the law added that religious and sexual discrimination was allowed if employers proved it was necessary for a particular job. As with the civil rights movement, passing a law was not enough to change attitudes and behaviour. In June 1966, a group of women, including Betty Friedan, set up the National Organisation for Women (NOW) as a women's civil rights group. Its aim was 'to bring women into full participation in American society now, with all its privileges and responsibilities, in truly equal partnership with men'.

Talk of 'women's liberation' began on campuses all over America. Radical men could be as prejudiced against equal rights for women as anyone else. At one radical meeting in Chicago, the man choosing speakers from the audience ignored women who raised their hands to speak. When a woman tried to take the microphone to speak, he patted her head and said, 'Cool down, little girl, we have more important things to talk about than women's problems.' Women in radical organisations set up local groups that spread ideas and developed their own radical magazines, but they did not form a national organisation. They felt they would work more effectively at a local level.

Opposition to liberation movements

Many men, and some women, opposed women's movements. There were many different reasons for opposition. Some opponents wanted women to stick to the role of homemaker. As late as 1970, new organisations, such as Happiness of Womanhood, were being formed to support the role of woman as homemaker. Others thought that women should be putting their energy into other movements (those against poverty or racism, for example).

Source A — Jo Freeman, *author of* The Politics of Women's Liberation, *describing her attempts to find work after university in 1967.*

After university, I wanted to be a journalist and worked unpaid for several months to put together a file of my work. When I went to look for a job as a news reporter, I was told, before they even opened my file, that the 5 per cent quota for women reporters was met, so they did not need a woman. During the next few months of answering job adverts and signing up at employment agencies, I experienced the many subtle and not-so-subtle forms of sex-discrimination for any job paying more than that of a secretary. Time and time again, I was told that, despite my abilities and the need for skilled workers, I could not be offered a good job because I would leave to get married (or have a baby, or just leave). At first, I tried to persuade them that I was different. Slowly, I realised that they didn't want to listen. The fact that I was a woman was all they saw.

Source B — Betty Friedan talking to reporters in April 1967. She is on a NOW demonstration urging the New York State Assembly to amend their laws to ban sexual discrimination as well as racial discrimination. Think about the sex of the reporters shown.

CIVIL RIGHTS FOR WOMEN

PUT SEX IN SECTION 1

NOW!

Source C

Information from the US Bureau of Statistics.

Census information for 1970 shows that:
- 38% of students at university were women
- 43% of women went out to work.

Of women working:
- 96% worked in other people's homes
- 69% did clerical work, such as filing and typing
- 14% were managers.

ResultsPlus
Watch out!

Many students make the mistake of thinking that a source which comes from the time period they are studying is more useful, or more reliable, than a secondary source, written later by a historian. Do not make this assumption. A secondary source based on a range of evidence collected by a historian can be just as useful or reliable as a primary source – or even more so. Always consider *where* a source comes from and *why* it has been produced and relate those factors back to the question you are being asked when you are judging how useful or reliable it is.

The contraceptive pill let women plan their pregnancies...

Margaret Chase Smith stood for President...

The Equal Pay Act was passed and sex discrimination was put into the Civil Rights Act...

... but they were hard to enforce.

Many cases were brought to court over equal opportunities...

...but she only got 27 votes.

...but only some states allowed its use, and usually only for married women.

President Johnson removed the limit on women in the military...

...but they could still not go into battle.

...but there was still discrimination everywhere else.

...but some women lecturers were sacked for teaching female equality.

Courses of women's history were introduced at some universities...

New York City banned 'men only' public facilities such as bars...

...but many failed (a firm in Indiana was allowed to stop women working on the factory floor because they had to lift over 35 lb – the average weight of a typewriter, which they moved all the time).

Activities

1   Compare Source C with Source D on page 71 (the previous set of census information). Write a sentence saying how things have changed between 1960 and 1970.

2   Read Source A. If Jo Freeman's experience was usual, what is unusual about the reporters in Source B? Do you think the photographer did this on purpose?

3   Read the thought bubbles above. They contain seven sentences split into 'heads and tails'. Match the sentence starters to the correct endings. Write out the completed sentences.

4   *Women's liberation had a long way to go in 1970 – it got hardly anywhere in the 1960s.* Write a paragraph explaining how far the sources support this statement.

In the Unit 3 examination, you will be required to answer five questions. We are going to look at question 5. The examiners think you need about 20 minutes to answer this question. It has the most marks and needs the most time. The number of marks helps you judge how much to write. We are going to use Sources B, C, D and E from the chapter in Key Topic 4 called 'Turn on, tune in, drop out' (pages 64–65) and Sources A, C and D from the chapter called 'How did students protest?' (pages 66–67).

ResultsPlus
Maximise your marks

Question 5

Examiner's tip: Question 5 will be a question that asks you how far the sources in the paper support a statement. You will need to use all the sources. Remember to keep focused on the statement and consider both support and the lack of it. Let's look at an example.

'Student protesters in the 1960s were just a bunch of kids rebelling against their parents' views.' How far do the sources support this statement? Use details from the sources and your own knowledge to explain your answer.' (16 marks)

Student answer	Examiner comment
Most of the sources don't support this idea. They suggest that students were protesting about issues that concerned them.	This is a level 1 answer. It only gives a very general answer to the question and does not refer to the content of any of the sources. Let's see what you would need to do to reach level 2.
Source D (page 65) shows one student clearly rejecting the values of the older generation: 'I reject everything my father stands for.' **But that is just one student, after all.** OR In Source C (on page 67) the authors of the textbook makes it clear that they are protesting about the war in Vietnam – it is the war and the injustice to the Vietnamese.	At level 2, answers consider the statement and produce relevant details from the sources to back up one side of the argument. The best kind of level 2 answer will also consider the limits of the sources (in bold in the example).

In Source D (page 65), it is really clear that this student is rejecting the values of the older generation: 'I reject everything my father stands for', so it is supporting the statement. In Source C, Bob Dylan suggests that parents will need to change or get out of the way – which is rejection: 'don't criticise what you can't understand', so that is a kind of support too. Source E (on page 65) and Sources A and C (pages 66-67) don't really give support in the same kind of way. They suggest it is Vietnam.

This is a level 3 answer. It focuses on the statement and uses detail from the sources to consider both support and the lack of it. However, a level 3 answer often concentrates on support or the lack of it, rather than giving a balanced consideration to both.

Some sources show rejection of their parents' generation by students. But that is not the same as that being the only thing that students protestors were doing, many of them were protesting over bigger issues. In Source D (page 65), the student rejects his father's values: 'I reject everything my father stands for' – this is clear support for the statement. In Source C, Dylan says parents will need to change or get out of the way – which is rejection: 'don't criticise what you can't understand'. **Source D is only one student, but Dylan was a voice for the whole generation – the song was very popular, many people must have agreed with the ideas in it. So this suggests there was a generation problem.** However, student protest was more than this, and Source E (page 65) doesn't support the idea that it was just a generation thing. It shows the political, not personal, reaction. **We know that many, if not most, student protests were against the war in Vietnam. Source E does not refer to students directly, but it shows one of the issues that we know they protested against.** And Sources C and D (page 67) both show they were protesting against Vietnam, that this was a big issue with them. So this supports Source E (from page 65). So I would say the sources show some support for the idea that students were rebelling against parents' views, but that they also show other issues that affected students – Vietnam and also authority/government in general.

To reach level 4 on this type of question, an answer needs to consider the evidence for and against the statement provided by the sources **and** how reliable or typical those sources are.

Welcome to exam zone

Revising for your exams can be a daunting prospect. Use this section of the book to get ideas, tips and practice to help you get the best results you can.

Zone In!

Have you ever become so absorbed in a task that it suddenly feels entirely natural? This is a feeling familiar to many athletes and performers: it's a feeling of being 'in the zone' that helps you focus and achieve your best.

Here are our top tips for getting in the zone with your revision.

- **Understand the exam process** and what revision you need to do. This will give you confidence but also help you to put things into proportion. Use the Planning Zone to create a revision plan.

- **Build your confidence** by using your revision time, not just to revise the information you need to know, but also to practise the skills you need for the examination. Try answering questions in timed conditions so that you're more prepared for writing answers in the exam.

- **Deal with distractions** by making a list of everything that might interfere with your revision and how you can deal with each issue. For example, revise in a room without a television, but plan breaks in your revision so that you can watch your favourite programmes.

- **Share your plan with friends and family** so that they know not to distract you when you want to revise. This will mean you can have more quality time with them when you aren't revising.

- **Keep healthy** by making sure you eat well and exercise, and by getting enough sleep. If your body is not in the right state, your mind won't be either – and staying up late to cram the night before the exam is likely to leave you too tired to do your best.

Planning Zone

The key to success in exams and revision often lies in the right planning, so that you don't leave anything until the last minute. Use these ideas to create your personal revision plan.

First, fill in the dates of your examinations. Check with your teacher when these are if you're not sure. Add in any regular commitments you have. This will help you get a realistic idea of how much time you have to revise.

Know your strengths and weaknesses and assign more time to topics you find difficult – don't be tempted to leave them until the last minute.

Create a revision 'checklist' using the Know Zone lists and use them to check your knowledge and skills.

Now fill in the timetable with sensible revision slots. Chunk your revision into smaller sections to make it more manageable and less daunting. Make sure you give yourself regular breaks and plan in different activities to provide some variety.

Keep to the timetable! Put your plan up somewhere visible so you can refer back to it and check that you are on track.

Know Zone

In this zone, you'll find checklists to help you review what you've learned and which areas you still need to work on.

Test your knowledge

Use these checklists to test your knowledge of the main areas for each topic. If you find gaps or weaknesses in your knowledge, refer back to the relevant pages of the book.

Key Topic 1

You should know about...

❏ The ideological clash behind the Cold War **see pages 9–11**

❏ How Cold War fear affected US foreign policy **see pages 9–11**

❏ The activities of HUAC and spread of the Red Scare **see pages 12–13**

❏ How McCarthy played on Cold War fears **see pages 14–15**

❏ The Rosenberg case and its impact **see pages 16–17**

❏ The fall of McCarthy **see pages 18–19**

Key Topic 2

You should know about...

❏ The aims and diversity of the civil rights movement **see pages 23–25**

❏ The tactics, especially non-violent tactics, of the civil rights movement **see pages 26–27**

❏ The causes, events and results of the Montgomery Bus Boycott **see pages 28–29**

❏ The role of Martin Luther King **see pages 28–29**

❏ Attempts to obtain civil rights, especially in education, via the constitution **see pages 30–31**

❏ The events at Little Rock **see pages 32–33**

❏ Sit-ins, freedom rides and violent opposition **see pages 34–35**

❏ Opposition groups, such as the Ku Klux Klan, and their methods **see pages 36–37**

Key Topic 3

You should know about...

❏ How views on segregation changed **see page 41**

❏ The events in Birmingham, Alabama **see pages 42–43**

❏ The march on Washington **see pages 44–45**

❏ Malcolm X and his message **see pages 46–47**

❏ Influences on Kennedy to promote civil rights **see pages 48–49**

Key Topic 3 continued

You should know about...

❏ The events of Freedom Summer **see pages 50–51**

❏ The Civil Rights Act of 1964 **see pages 52–53**

❏ The Voter Rights Act of 1965 **see pages 52–53**

❏ Some aims and tactics of Black Power groups **see pages 54–55**

❏ Riots in cities, 1965–68 **see pages 56–57**

❏ King's assassination **see pages 58–59**

❏ King's place in the civil rights movement **see pages 58–59**

Key Topic 4

You should know about...

❏ How the USA changed after the Second World War **see page 63**

❏ Reasons for student protest in the 1960s **see pages 64–65**

❏ Types of student protest **see pages 66–67**

❏ The increase in violence by protesters and police **see pages 66–67**

❏ The events and impact of the shootings at Kent State **see pages 68–69**

❏ Views of the role of women in the 1950s and early 1960s **see pages 70–71**

❏ Position of women in the workforce **see pages 70–71**

❏ Groups that campaigned for women's liberation **see pages 72–73**

Working with sources

Remember, however, that this unit is not just about recalling historical information: you need to be able to interpret and make judgements about historical sources.

As you've studied each topic, you'll have built up a range of skills for working with sources. The table below lists the main areas you should now feel confident in and shows where each is covered in the book. Refer back to those pages during your revision to check and practise your source skills.

	Key topic 1	Key topic 2	Key topic 3	Key topic 4
Making inferences from sources	Page 9	Pages 23 and 26	Pages 50 and 54	Pages 64 and 70
Considering the purpose of a source	Page 12	Pages 28 and 30	Pages 42 and 56	
Cross-referencing sources	Page 14		Pages 48, 52 and 58	Pages 66 and 72
Evaluating the utility or reliability of sources	Page 16	Pages 34 and 36	Page 46	Page 68
Evaluating a hypothesis	Page 18	Page 32	Page 44	

Exam Zone Unit 3C practice exam paper

Here is a practice paper for your Unit 3C exam. The sources that you need to read to answer these questions are provided on pages 80–81. In Unit 3 you need to answer all five questions. Each question will tell you which source or sources you need to read and refer to. The number of marks available for each question is given on the right. Remember that the Unit 3 exam lasts 1 hour 15 minutes. Plan your time accordingly!

Question 1
Study Source A
What can you learn about the civil rights movement from Source A? (6)

Question 2
Study Source B and use your own knowledge.
What was the purpose of this speech? Use details of the source and your own knowledge to explain the answer. (8)

Question 3
Study Sources A, B and C.
How far do these sources agree about the tactics used by the civil rights movement in the 1960s? Explain your answer. (10)

Question 4
Study Sources D and E.
How useful are Sources D and E as evidence of the divide in the civil rights movement? Explain your answer. (10)

Question 5
Study all the sources and use your own knowledge.
'The civil rights movement became increasingly militant in the 1960s.'
How far do the sources in this paper support this statement? Use details from the sources and your own knowledge to explain the answer. (16)

Exam Zone

Background information

There were changes in the civil rights movement in the 1960s. There was a growing frustration with the lack of progress made by non-violent campaigning. Many black civil rights campaigners began to feel that non-violent direct action was failing to change laws or get civil rights laws enforced. There was a growing feeling of militancy, a growing feeling that the time had come for violent action. There was also a change from seeing civil rights as a Southern issue to one of seeing it as a US-wide issue. Large scale riots broke out in various northern cities from 1963 on.

So did everyone become more militant?

Source A   A photograph of marchers singing at a civil rights demonstration. From a series of photos taken for an article in *Life* magazine about the Selma to Montgomery March in March 1965.

Source B   From a speech given in New York by Malcolm X on 8 April 1964.

1964 will be America's hottest year; a year of much racial violence and much bloodshed. But this time the blood won't be going to flow all only on one side. The new generation of black people that have grown up in this country are forming the opinion that if there is to be bleeding, it should be reciprocal – bleeding on both sides. The black man has ceased to turn the other cheek, has ceased to be non-violent.

Source C   Said by Martin Luther King to a TV reporter in 1968, after a press conference on the Poor People's campaign that King took part in.

I don't know if you are aware of it, but you keep driving people like me, who are non-violent, into saying more and more militant things. If we don't say things militantly enough for you, we don't get on the evening news. And who does? The militants, that's who. By doing this, you are, first of all, selecting the militant black leaders to be civil rights leaders, because everyone sees them on your television programmes. And secondly, you are making violence the way to publicise our cause.

Exam Zone

Source D   Two members of the Black Panther Movement being given permission to go into the Californian State Assembly, having agreed not to disturb the peace, on 2 May 1967.

Source E   From a speech given in Atlanta, Georgia, by Martin Luther King on 16 August 1967.

Now, let me say we must reaffirm our commitment to nonviolence. And I want to stress this. The futility of violence in the struggle for racial justice has been tragically shown in all the recent Negro riots. There is something painfully sad about a riot: screaming youngsters and angry adults fighting hopelessly against impossible odds. Occasionally, Negroes say the riots in various cities represented effective civil rights action. But they always end up with stumbling words when asked what gains have been won. At best, the riots have won a little additional anti-poverty money from frightened government officials and a few water sprinklers to cool the children of the ghettos. It is like improving food in the prison while the people stay behind bars. Nowhere have the riots won concrete improvement such as have the organized protest demonstrations.

Source F   From an article about the impact of Martin Luther King in the *Anniston Star* newspaper on Martin Luther King Day, 19 January 2009. The extract refers to the march shown in Source B and its photographer.

No one understood the power of vivid images better than King, and he fretted over every lost opportunity. At one point in Selma, Flip Schulke of *Life* magazine saw (Sheriff Jim) Clark's posse shove children to the ground. He stopped taking photographs and began pushing the men away. King heard about the incident and reminded Schulke about his 'duty as a photographer.' [to record violent reaction to non-violent demonstrators].

Don't Panic Zone

As the day of the exam gets closer, many students tend to go into panic mode, either working long hours without really giving their brain a chance to absorb information, or giving up and staring blankly at the wall.

Look over your revision notes and go through the checklists to remind yourself of the main areas you need to know about. Don't try to cram in too much new information at the last minute and don't stay up late revising – you'll do better if you get a good night's sleep.

Exam Zone

What to expect in the exam paper

You will have 1 hour and 15 minutes in the examination. There will be five questions and you should answer all of these. There will be between six and eight sources in a separate source booklet; some of these will be written and some illustrations.

Question 1 is an inference question worth 6 marks. It will ask what a source is suggesting, usually phrased as 'What can you learn from Source X'? You should spend about 10 minutes on this question. For an example, see page 20.

Question 2 is an evaluation question worth 8 marks. It will ask you about the purpose of the source, for example 'Why was the source produced?' or 'Why was this photograph used?' For an example, see page 21.

Question 3 is worth 10 marks and involves comparing or cross-referencing up to three sources. The question will usually be in the form 'Do these sources support the view that…?', 'How far do these sources agree about…?' or 'Do Sources A and B support Source C about…?' For an example see page 38.

Question 4 is worth 10 marks and asks you to evaluate the utility or reliability of two sources. For example, 'How useful or how reliable are Sources D and E?' For an example, see page 60.

Question 5 is a judgement question worth 16 marks. It will start with a statement and then ask 'How far do the sources in this paper support this statement? Use details from the sources and your own knowledge.' For an example see page 74.

Meet the exam paper

This diagram shows the front cover of the exam paper. These instructions, information and advice will always appear on the front of the paper. It is worth reading it carefully now. Check you understand it and ask your teacher about anything you are not sure of.

Print your surname here, and your other names afterwards. This is an additional safeguard to ensure that the exam board awards the marks to the right candidate.

Here you fill in the school's exam number.

The Unit 3 exam lasts 1 hour 15 minutes. Plan your time accordingly.

Make sure that you answer all questions.

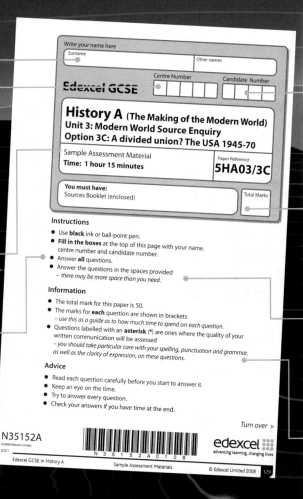

Here you fill in your personal exam number. Take care to write it accurately.

In this box, the examiner will write the total marks you have achieved in the exam paper.

Don't feel that you have to fill the answer space provided. Everybody's handwriting varies, so a long answer from you may take up as much space a short answer from someone else.

Remember that in question 5 the quality of your written communication will be assessed. Take time to check your spelling, punctuation and grammar and to make sure that you have expressed yourself clearly.

In Unit 3 you need to answer all five questions on the paper.

Each question will tell you which source or sources you need to read in the sources booklet.

The number of marks available for each question is given on the right.

The sources booklet will provide you with some background information that will help you to put the sources in context.

Read the detail about the provenance and date of each source carefully before studying the source.

Answer all questions.

This question paper is about the Civil Rights movement.

Look carefully at the background information and Sources A to F in the Sources Booklet and then answer Questions 1 to 5 which follow.

1   **Study Source A.**

What can you learn from Source A about events at Little Rock High School in 1957?   (6)

The live question paper will contain one further page of lines.

(Total for Question 1 = 6 marks)

130   Edexcel GCSE in History A   Sample Assessment Materials   © Edexcel Limited 2008

Background information

There was much progress in the campaign for civil rights for black US citizens in the years after 1945. Some historians claim that it was the Montgomery Bus Boycott which did most to encourage such progress. Other historians argue that other factors were equally or more important.

So, what was the main reason for progress in civil rights in the years 1945-60?

Source A: Arkansas Governor Orval Faubus being interviewed in 1980 about the events at Little Rock High School in 1957.

I placed a small force of National Guardsmen on duty at Little Rock to preserve the peace. I could not wait for violence. I then promptly complied with the federal order to remove the National Guard. The next day there was disorder and the president sent 1,100 troops to Little Rock to escort the students into school. I am fully convinced that my handling of the situation helped to prevent violence and disorder.

Source B: Official BBC report, September 1957, on the events at Little Rock High School.

Nine black students have finally been able to attend Central High School in Little Rock, Arkansas. But they had to be surrounded by more than 1,000 troops, sent by President Eisenhower, to protect them against racist whites. The troops arrived last night and took over from local police after three weeks of disturbances. The students had to walk through a cordon to get to the school building. Outside, about 1,500 whites demonstrated, some violently, and at least seven were arrested.

136   Edexcel GCSE in History A   Sample Assessment Materials   © Edexcel Limited 2008

Zone Out

This section provides answers to the most common questions students have about what happens after they complete their exams. For much more information, visit www.examzone.co.uk.

When will my results be published?

Results for GCSE summer examinations are issued in the third week of August. January exam results are issued in March.

Can I get my results online?

Visit www.resultsplusdirect.co.uk, where you will find detailed student results information including the 'Edexcel Gradeometer' which demonstrates how close you were to the nearest grade boundary.

I haven't done as well as I expected. What can I do now?

First of all, talk to your teacher. After all the teaching that you have had, and the tests and internal examinations you have done, he/she is the person who best knows what grade you are capable of achieving. Take your results slip to your subject teacher, and go through the information on it in detail. If you both think that there is something wrong with the result, the school or college can apply to see your completed examination paper and then, if necessary, ask for a re-mark immediately.

Bear in mind that the original mark can be confirmed or lowered, as well as raised, as a result of a re-mark. After a re-mark, the only way to improve your grade is to take the examination again. Your school or college Examinations Officer can tell you when you can do that.

I achieved a higher mark for the same unit last time. Can I use that result?

Yes. The higher score is the one that goes towards your overall grade. You do not need to ask Edexcel to take into account a previous result. This will be done automatically so you can be assured that all your best unit results have gone into calculating your overall grade.

How many times can I resit a unit?

You may resit a unit once prior to claiming certification for the qualification. The best available result for each contributing unit will count towards the final grade. If you wish to resit after you have completed all the assessment requirements of the course, you will have to retake at least 40% of the assessment requirements (that means two units). Please note that if you take a resit as one of the two units in your final assessment, the score you get will be counted – even if your original score was higher.

Glossary

Term	Definition
ballot	Vote.
Baptist	A Protestant Christian who believes that people cannot be baptised in a ceremony to join that religion until they are adults and old enough to understand the promise they are making.
bigotry	Believing something unreasonable; an example of bigotry in this unit would be believing that black people are not as good as white people.
boycott	To refuse to use a service if it does something you consider wrong (e.g. discriminates against black people, mistreats animals).
bribe	The promise of money or something else a person wants in return for them doing something.
capitalism	A way of running the economy where individuals own businesses, fund them and take the profits from them.
capitalist	A person who believes in capitalism. When applied to a country, it means a country run according to capitalist ideas.
censure	Disapproval; a motion of censure in political terms is a public announcement that everyone else in that political group disapproves of what has been said/done.
communism	A way of running the economy (or a country) where the state owns all businesses, funds them, takes the profits from them and supports all those who are part of the economy or country.
communist	A person who believes in communism. When applied to a country, it means a country run according to communist ideas.
direct action	Visible actions by groups that want to make political changes, such as boycotts and protest marches, which aim to gain publicity and confront the government with the problem without resorting to violence.

Term	Definition
espionage	Spying: giving information about a country to another country, having found out the information and passed it on secretly.
federal laws	The federal government in the USA makes the laws that affect the whole country; individual states also make their own laws that just affect what goes on in that state.
freedom ride	Riding on public transport to desegregate it or the facilities at its stations.
infiltrated	If a person has infiltrated a group or organisation they have joined it by not telling the truth about themselves, in order to find out about it or harm it.
lynch	To lynch a person is to execute them, usually by hanging, for a supposed crime without a legal trial.
militant	Believing in violent action.
paranoia	Unreasonable distrust and fear of something.
picketing	Demonstrating outside a place that does something you consider wrong (e.g. discriminates against black people) and asking others not to use it.
plaintiff	The person who has taken a case to court.
racism	Prejudice against people of a different race.
sabotage	Deliberately stopping something from working properly.
segregation	Within civil rights, having different facilities and living areas for black and white people.
sit-in	To sit down in a place and refuse to move as a protest.
unconstitutional	Against the constitution – the rules that govern the country.

Acknowledgements

Pearson Education Limited
Edinburgh Gate
Harlow
Essex
CM20 2JE
England
© Pearson Education 2009

The right of Jane Shuter to be identified as the author of this work has been asserted by her in accordance with the Copyright, Designs and Patents Act 1988.

ISBN 978-1-84690-552-0

Designed by eMC Design Ltd

The publishers are grateful to Jenny Clifton and Simon Hall for their contributions to the book.

Artwork by Design Tribe

First edition 2009
Fourth impression 2010
Printed in Malaysia, KHL-CTP

The publisher and authors wish to thank the following for their kind permission to reproduce their photographs:

(Key: b-bottom; c-centre; l-left; r-right; t-top)
Bridgeman Art Library Ltd: Colin Bootman 29; **CONELRAD.com:** Conelrad 10; **Corbis:** Bettmann 8, 11, 14, 15, 16, 17, 23, 26, 27, 28, 30, 33, 35, 45, 46, 47, 48, 51, 53, 81; David J. & Janice L. Frent Collection 24, 54; Steve Schapiro 40, 50; Flip Schulke 37, 80; Leif Skoogfors 7, 62, 67; **Getty Images:** CBS Photo Archive 57; John Filo 69; Hulton Archive 52; **Library of Congress:** A. Philip Randolph Educational Fund / LC-DIG-ppmsca-08112 59; LC-USZ62-122632 72; LC-USZC4-6624 55; Visual Materials from the NAACP Records / LC-USZ62-125549 41; Visual Materials from the NAACP Records / LC-USZ62-84483 22, 25; **Copyright by Bill Mauldin (1963):** Courtesy of the Bill Mauldin Estate LLC 49; **PA Photos:** AP / Bill Hudson 43; AP / Fred Blackwell 34; **The Herb Block Foundation:** 6, 13, 19, 31, 65; **TopFoto:** HIP / Land of Lost Content 71; Topham Picturepoint 63

Cover images: *Front:* **Corbis:** Flip Schulke

All other images © Pearson Education

Picture Research by: Sarah Purtill

Every effort has been made to trace the copyright holders and we apologise in advance for any unintentional omissions. We would be pleased to insert the appropriate acknowledgement in any subsequent edition of this publication.

We are grateful to the following for permission to reproduce copyright material:

Alabama Department of Archives & History for an extract paraphrased from "bus riding rules" www.africanamericanstudies.buffalo.edu/ANNOUNCE/vra/montgomery/doc3.html; Blackwell Publishing, Ltd for a poem from *The Civil Rights Movement* by Jack E Davis copyright © Blackwells 2001. Reproduced with permission of Blackwell Publishing, Ltd; Carol Mann Agency for an extract from an interview with Elizabeth Eckford, published in *Witnesses to Freedom* by Belinda Rochelle copyright © 1997 by Belinda Rochelle. Reprinted with permission of the Carol Mann Agency; CNN for an extract from an interview with Rennie Davis in November 1996, from http://edition.cnn.com/SPECIALS/cold.war/episodes/13/interviews/davis/ reproduced with permission; CORE-Congress of Racial Equality for an extract from www.core-online.org, reproduced with permission; Professor Jerry H Farber for an extract from "August, 1965" by Jerry Farber published in *Reporting C Rights*, copyright © Jerry Farber; Hachette Book Group USA for an extract from *Many are the Crimes* by Ellen Wolf Schrecker, copyright © 1998, by permission of Little, Brown & Company; Bruce Hartford for an extract from the Civil Rights Movement Veterans' website www.crmvet.org, reproduced with permission; KTWU for an extract from an interview with Linda Brown. Transcript of program produced by KTWU/Channel 11, Topeka, Kansas 3 May 2004, reproduced with permission; Little, Brown Book Group and Hachette Book Group USA for an extract from *The Autobiography of Martin Luther King, Jr* edited by Clayborne Carson, 2001 by NULL Intellectual Properties Mgmt, copyright © Little, Brown Book Group Ltd and by permission of Grand Central Publishing; Los Angeles Times for an extract from a report about the night of 15 August 1965 in Los Angeles, the *Los Angeles Times*, August 16 1965, reproduced by permission; NCRRC for an extract from the National Committee to Reopen the Rosenberg Case http://rosenbergtrial.org/, reproduced with permission; The Dr. Huey P. Newton Foundation for an extract from "The Ten Point Plan" http://www.blackpanther.org/TenPoint.htm, reproduced with permission; The Orion Publishing Group Ltd and Curtis Brown, Ltd for an extract from *The Feminine Mystique* by Betty Friedan copyright © 1997, 1991, 1974, 1963 by Betty Friedan published by Victor Gollancz, an imprint of The Orion Publishing Group Ltd, reproduced by permission of The Orion Publishing Group Ltd and Curtis Brown, Ltd; Palgrave Macmillan for extracts from *The Civil Rights Movement* by W T M Riches copyright © 1997. Reproduced with permission of Palgrave Macmillan; Penguin Group (USA) Inc. for extracts from *Freedom's Children* edited by Ellen Levine, copyright © 1993 by Ellen Levine. Used by permission of G.P. Putnam's Sons, A Division of Penguin Young Readers Group, A Member of Penguin Group (USA) Inc., 345 Hudson Street, New York, NY 10014. All rights reserved; The Random House Group Ltd; Random House, Inc and The Doe Coover Agency for extracts from *Voices of Freedom: An Oral History of the Civil Rights Movement from the 1950's through the 1980's* by Henry Hampton and Steve Fayer. Published by Bantam Books copyright © 1990 Blackside, Inc. Used by permission of Blackside, Inc; The Random House Group Ltd, and Bantom Books, a division of Random House, Inc; Sony/ATV Music Publishing (UK) Ltd for the lyric reproduction of "The Times They are a Changin'". Lyrics by Bob Dylan copyright © 1963; renewed 1991 Special Rider Music. Administered by Sony/ATV Music Publishing. All rights reserved. Used by permission; Swarthmore College and William Morris Agency, LLC for an extract from *Kent State: What Happened and Why* by James Michener copyright © 1971 by James Michener. Reprinted by permission of William Morris Agency, LLC on behalf of the Author; and Writers House for extracts from a letter written by Martin Luther King while in prison in Birmingham, Alabama 1963; the speech "I have a dream" by Martin Luther King, Washington 28 August 1963; an extract speech given by Martin Luther King at the start of the voter registration campaign in Alabama 1965; a quote by Martin Luther King; an extract from a speech by Martin Luther King, Atlanta, Georgia 16 August 1967; and a quote by Martin Luther King to a TV reporter 1968, after a press conference on the Poor People's campaign that King took part in. Reprinted by arrangement with The Heirs to the Estate of Martin Luther King Jr., c/o Writers House as agent for the proprietor New York, NY. Copyright 1963 Dr. Martin Luther King Jr; copyright renewed 1991 Coretta Scott King.

In some instances we have been unable to trace the owners of copyright material and we would appreciate any information that would enable us to do so.